Law and Employment

Discrimination

After studying at Sussex University and Trinity Hall, Cambridge, **Linda Clarke** taught law at Essex University. She is qualified as a barrister, and is currently a Lecturer in Law at the Centre for Legal Studies at Sussex University. She is an Associate Adviser to the Industrial Society and writes regularly on employment law.

Law and Employment series

General editor: Olga Aikin

The law relating to employment can seem labyrinthine – but with today's escalating number of legal claims, managers ignore it at their peril.

Managers must be able to construct sound yet flexible and progressive employment policies built on firm legal foundations. This important new series will enable them to meet the challenge. It forms a superbly practical and, above all, accessible source of reference on employment practice and law.

The IPD has specially commissioned Olga Aikin – one of the UK's foremost authorities on employment law, a qualified barrister and well-known legal writer – to steer the project. Individual titles have been written by leading legal experts and human resource practitioners. Together they provide a unique combination of up-to-date legal guidance with in-depth advice on current employment issues.

Other titles in the series include:

Contracts
Olga Aikin

Discipline
Philip James and David Lewis

Industrial Tribunals
2nd edition
Roger Greenhalgh

Redundancy
Alan Fowler

The Institute of Personnel and Development is the leading publisher of books and reports for personnel and training professionals and students and for all those concerned with the effective management and development of people at work. For full details of all our titles please telephone the Publishing Department on 0181 263 3387.

Law and Employment series

Discrimination

Linda Clarke

Second Edition

INSTITUTE OF PERSONNEL AND DEVELOPMENT

© Linda Clarke 1994, 1995

First published 1994
Second edition 1995

Typesetting by The Comp-Room, Aylesbury, Buckinghamshire
and printed in Great Britain by
The Cromwell Press Ltd, Broughton Gifford, Wiltshire

British Library Cataloguing in Publication Data
A catalogue record for this book is available from the British Library

    ISBN 0 85292 625 1 2nd edition
    (ISBN 0-85292-528-X 1st edition)

The views expressed in the book are the author's own, and may not necessarily reflect those of the IPD.

INSTITUTE OF PERSONNEL
AND DEVELOPMENT

IPD House, Camp Road, London SW19 4UX
Tel: 0181 971 9000   Fax: 0181 263 3333
Registered office as above. Registered Charity No. 1038333
A company limited by guarantee. Registered in England No. 2931892

Contents

General editor's foreword

This series is essentially a user's guide to employment law and good employment practice. The objective is to provide managers, trade unionists and the employees themselves with a basic understanding of the legal rules and basic principles which affect the employment relationship. There is no intention of turning everyone into a lawyer, but today a little knowledge of employment law is far from dangerous and a fair amount can be a positive advantage.

In the past thirty years we have moved away from a situation in which the law relating to employment could be ignored, in which legal actions were few and far between, into one in which the number of legal claims is increasing and in which the law is becoming far more complex. But this does not mean that it is a matter for lawyers, or, even when lawyers are essential, that the decisions have to be left to them alone. Lawyers and consultants can only advise. Business decisions have to be made by managers; employees have to decide whether there is an advantage in suing. The law is rarely 100 per cent certain and the ultimate decision has to be made by the client.

The law is not enough. The purpose of the law is to set minima and devise means of dealing with the fall-back situation when the parties cannot reach a solution. Good employment relations demand far more than mere compliance with legal requirements. They require an understanding of the nature of the relationship between employer and employee and how the manager manages it.

This series is concerned not only with the practical application of the law but also with the problems and issues which arise before, during and after employment. For this reason it starts with the practical situation and explains the law relating to it, the pitfalls and advantages, and suggests approaches which may be helpful.

The authors are all experts in their fields and combine legal knowledge with practical expertise.

Olga Aikin

List of abbreviations

AC	Appeal Cases
ACAS	Advisory Conciliation and Arbitration Service
All ER	All England Law Reports
COIT	Central Office of Industrial Tribunals
CRE	Commission for Racial Equality
DP(E)A	Disabled Persons (Employment) Act
DRO	Disablement Resettlement Officer
DSS	Department of Social Security
EAT	Employment Appeal Tribunal
ECJ	European Court of Justice
EOC	Equal Opportunities Commission
EOR	Equal Opportunities Review
EOR-DCLD	Equal Opportunities Review – Discrimination Case Law Digest
EP(C)A	Employment Protection (Consolidation) Act
EqPA	Equal Pay Act
GOQ	Genuine Occupational Qualification
ICR	Industrial Cases Reports
IDS	Incomes Data Services Ltd
ILEA	Inner London Education Authority
IRLB	Industrial Relations Law Bulletin
IRLIB	Industrial Relations Legal Information Bulletin
IRLR	Industrial Relations Law Reports
IT	Industrial Tribunal
JES	Job Evaluation Study
MA	Maternity Allowance
MLP	Maternity Leave Period
NAT	National Aids Trust
QB	Queen's Bench
RRA	Race Relations Act
SDA	Sex Discrimination Act
SMP	Statutory Maternity Pay
SSP	Statutory Sick Pay
TLR	Times Law Reports
TULR(C)A	Trade Union and Labour Relations (Consolidation) Act
TURERA	Trade Union Reform and Employment Rights Act
WLR	Weekly Law Reports

This series has been produced for instruction and information. Whilst every care has been taken in the preparation of the books, they should not be used to provide precedents for drawing up contracts or policies. All terms should be carefully considered in the light of the prevailing law and the needs of the organisation. When in doubt, it is recommended that professional legal advice is sought.

For the purposes of this book the law is as stated on 31 October 1995.

Chapter 1
Introduction

Discrimination at work involves treating some people less favourably than others on the basis of characteristics that are irrelevant to their ability to do the job in question. This may be due to an employer relying on prejudiced stereotypes – that women with young children are unreliable, that black people are lazy, that disabled people would not fit in – rather than looking at the individual before them; but discriminatory practices may also arise because an employer fails to take account of real differences between individuals – for example, that women do become pregnant, or that disabled workers may need extra facilities. In the UK, the law requires employers not to discriminate in certain contexts, and it is the purpose of this book to provide a clear and comprehensive guide to the law in this area.

However, it can be argued that it is not enough for an employer to aim simply to remain within the law, since non-discrimination also produces business advantages. During the late 1980s there was much talk of the 'demographic time bomb'. It was estimated that the number of young people coming into the labour market would fall by some 25 per cent during the 1990s, making it imperative for employers to draw on previously untapped groups of potential workers, notably women, in order to find sufficient employees. Employers began to think about childcare schemes and workplace nurseries in an effort to recruit and retain women. However, although the demographic time bomb may still be ticking away, its effects have been masked by the recession, and many of the nurseries that opened so publicly have quietly closed.

Nevertheless, non-discrimination still makes good business sense, rather than being just a vague social duty. Employees are an employer's key resource, and it is important to recruit – and keep – the right person for the job, and to train and promote people to the best of their abilities. Employers who discriminate, by allowing irrelevant considerations such as a person's sex or race to affect employment decisions, will not be getting the best person for the job. Employers who fail to recognise differences between individuals which may require extra training or flexibility will not be making the most of their workforce's potential. In the end, employers who take equal opportunities at work seriously will benefit.

Non-discrimination – or equality – can mean equal treatment, equality of opportunity, or equal results; the law in the UK requires only that

1

employers treat similarly situated employees equally. The primary focus of anti-discrimination law is discrimination on the grounds of sex and race. There are also more limited legislative provisions covering disability, ex-offenders, trade union members and religion (in Northern Ireland only). It is important to realise that almost all forms of positive discrimination are unlawful: an employer, with very limited exceptions, cannot decide to employ a woman because of her sex, or anyone because of their race, even though women or ethnic minorities may, in the past, have been gravely under-represented in the employer's workforce. However, an employer who is serious about equal opportunities will want to go beyond what the law requires in terms of non-discrimination. It is possible for employers to develop effective policies which promote equal opportunities, or even positive action programmes, without being guilty of positive discrimination.

European Community law

Employers obviously need to be aware of the law on discrimination. However, since the UK joined the EEC in 1973, European law has become increasingly important in this area, and it is essential that employers keep abreast of European developments. Although EC law is currently only of direct relevance to sex discrimination, the European Commission is showing considerable interest in the issue of racial discrimination.

Reference will be made throughout this book to EC provisions and cases decided in the European Court of Justice (ECJ), and it is important to understand the effect of different kinds of European provision.

Treaty provisions

Any Article of an EC Treaty which creates rights enforceable by individuals has *direct effect*. This means that it can be used by *individuals* to bring legal action in the national courts of Member States. So a woman in the UK can bring an equal pay claim against her employer by relying on Article 119 of the Treaty of Rome. She does not have to use the Equal Pay Act 1970.

Directives

Directives operate as instructions to Member States to introduce legislation that gives effect to the result envisaged by the Directive. There is usually a time limit by which Member States should implement the Directive: for example, the Council Directive 92/85 on Pregnant Workers had to be implemented by 19 October 1994.

Individuals can only rely on Directives to enforce rights against their

employer if the employer is an organ of the State. This is because it
would be wrong to allow the State to rely on its own failure to implement a Directive if this denies an individual rights guaranteed under that
Directive. An organ of the State has been widely defined as 'a body,
whatever its legal form, which has been made responsible by the State
for providing a public service under the control of the State and has for
that purpose special powers beyond those which result in the normal
rules applicable in relations between individuals'.[1] So in *Marshall* v.
Southampton and South-West Hampshire Area Health Authority (1986)[2]
the ECJ ruled that a woman could rely on the Equal Treatment Directive
76/207 to establish that it was unlawful for the Health Authority to have
set differing retirement ages for men and women employees.

However, even where the employee works for a private employer,
Directives are still important. Firstly, it is now well established that
judges in the UK will interpret UK legislation so as to accord with the
meaning and purpose of any relevant Directive, unless the UK law is
unambiguous and contradicts the Directive. Secondly, in the *Francovitch*
case[3] the ECJ held that where a Member State has failed to implement a
Directive, an individual may be entitled to damages from the State if
three conditions are met:

- the result required by the Directive includes conferring rights for the
  benefit of the individual
- the content of those rights can be determined by reference to the provisions of the Directive
- there is a causal link between the breach of the obligation by the State
  and the damage suffered by the individuals affected.

In these circumstances, it would be possible for private-sector employees
to claim damages from the UK Government where they have suffered
some loss as a result of the Government's failure to implement or fully
implement an EC Directive.

It is also possible to seek judicial review where Community law is
incompatible with domestic law. In *R.* v. *Secretary of State for
Employment ex parte Equal Opportunities Commission* (1994)[4] the
Equal Opportunities Commission (EOC) argued that the hours threshold
contained in the EP(C)A 1978 was contrary to Community law as it indirectly discriminated against women. The House of Lords held that the
EOC was entitled to bring the action, and further held that the hours
provisions were incompatible with Community law. As a result, the
Government was forced to introduce the Employment Protection (Part-
time Employees) Regulations 1995: the Regulations removed all hours
qualifications for unfair dismissal, redundancy, maternity rights and
other statutory rights.

The right to seek judicial review also enables individuals to challenge the legality of legislation on the basis of incompatibility with Community law. In *R.* v. *Secretary of State for Employment ex parte Seymour-Smith and Perez* (1995)[5] the Court of Appeal held that two women dismissed by private-sector employers after less than two years' service were entitled to seek a declaration that the two-year service qualification for claiming unfair dismissal was incompatible with Community legislation on sex discrimination. The Court of Appeal accepted that considerably fewer women than men could meet the requirement of two years' continuous service, and that the Government had failed to justify the requirement.

Time limits for bringing actions based on European law

There is considerable confusion over what time limits apply to cases brought on the basis of European law, and to what extent decisions such as *R.* v. *Secretary of State for Employment ex parte EOC* allow for retrospective claims. In *Emmott* v. *Minister for Social Welfare and A-G* (1991)[6] the ECJ held that it was for Member States to determine what time limits are appropriate for claims brought under Community law, as long as such time limits are not less favourable than those applying to similar claims under domestic law, and as long as the time limits do not make it virtually impossible for individuals to exercise their rights under Community law. But where a claim is based upon a Directive that has not been properly implemented into domestic law, the time limit begins to run only when the State has implemented the Directive fully.

The *Emmott* principle concerns rights contained in Directives. In *Biggs* v. *Somerset County Council* (1995)[7] the Employment Appeal Tribunal (EAT) held that the same principle did not apply to claims brought on the basis of directly effective Community legislation such as Article 119. So a part-time science teacher dismissed in 1976 was not allowed to claim unfair dismissal within three months of the decision of the House of Lords in *R.* v. *Secretary of State ex parte EOC*, as the three-month time limit for unfair dismissal ran from the date of her dismissal: it would have been possible for her to have brought her case in 1976 on the basis that the hours threshold was incompatible with Community law. This rather unrealistic decision is certain to be appealed.

Key points

- Equal opportunities make good business sense.
- Positive discrimination is unlawful, but positive action is not.
- Employers should always be aware of developments in European law.

References

1 *Foster* v. *British Gas* [1990] IRLR 353
2 [1986] QB 401
3 *Francovitch* v. *Italian Republic* [1992] IRLR 84
4 [1994] IRLR 176
5 [1995] IRLR 464
6 [1991] IRLR 387
7 [1995] IRLR 452

` Chapter 2
Sex discrimination

The Equal Pay Act 1970 and the Sex Discrimination Act 1975 are the two major legal provisions covering sex discrimination in employment. The Equal Pay Act 1970 (EqPA) covers all the contractual aspects of discrimination, while the Sex Discrimination Act 1975 (SDA) is designed to cover non-contractual discriminatory treatment. The SDA 1975 also outlaws sex discrimination in education and in the provision of goods and services. Although it is frequently stated that the two Acts are complementary and are designed to be read as 'a single comprehensive code',[1] the Acts operate separately and in significantly different ways. The Equal Opportunities Commission (EOC) has recommended that the two Acts should be integrated into an Equal Treatment Act, covering all aspects of discrimination at work.[2]

The SDA 1975 was passed following a growth in concern over, and interest in, women's rights, particularly in the light of experience in the US. Further stimulus arose from the UK's joining the EEC in 1973: the Treaty of Rome, in Article 119, provided that men and women were entitled to equal pay for equal work, and in 1975 the Equal Pay Directive was passed, followed in 1976 by the Equal Treatment Directive. European law and the decisions of the European Court of Justice (ECJ) have had an enormous influence on discrimination law in the UK, and will continue to do so in the foreseeable future.

It is now also possible for the EOC to challenge legislation in the United Kingdom courts, on the grounds that it is incompatible with European law. In a landmark decision, *R.* v. *Secretary of State for Employment ex parte Equal Opportunities Commission* (1994)[3] the House of Lords ruled that the requirement that part-timers (those working less than 16 hours per week) had to work for five years for the same employer before becoming entitled to statutory rights to bring an unfair dismissal complaint and to a redundancy payment was incompatible with Community law, as it amounted to indirect sex discrimination. The Government introduced the Employment Protection (Part-time Employees) Regulations 1995 with the result that all workers, regardless of the number of hours worked in a week, are entitled to the same statutory rights.

6

What is discrimination?

The SDA 1975 covers both direct and indirect discrimination. It is worth noting here that, although the provisions are generally worded in terms of discrimination against women, section 2(1) states:

> Section 1, and the provisions . . . relating to sex discrimination against women, are to be read as applying equally to the treatment of men.

Direct discrimination

Direct discrimination is defined by section 1(1)(a) as follows:

> A person discriminates against a woman in any circumstances relevant to the purposes of any provision of this Act if –
> > (a) on the ground of her sex he treats her less favourably than he treats or would treat a man.

It is also unlawful to discriminate against married people of either sex. This is defined by section 3(1)(a) as occurring if:

> on the ground of [an employee's] marital status [an employer] treats that person less favourably than he treats or would treat an unmarried person of the same sex.

However, it is worth noting that, although the SDA 1975 only prohibits discrimination against married people, the EC Equal Treatment Directive 76/207 prohibits discrimination on the grounds of 'marital or family status' and so would include single people.

In *R.* v. *Ministry of Defence ex parte Smith and others*[4] the High Court was asked to consider whether the Ministry of Defence's policy that homosexual men and women should not be allowed to serve in the armed forces was contrary to the Equal Treatment Directive. It was argued by the dismissed servicemen and women that the word 'sex' in the Directive included discrimination on grounds of sexuality. The High Court rejected this argument, holding that the word 'sex' meant discrimination on grounds of gender, not sexual orientation. Only if an employer refused to employ gay men, but not lesbians, would there be discrimination on grounds of sex.

Direct discrimination involves two key elements:

- There must be *less favourable treatment*.
- The treatment must be *because of sex or marital status*.

It is important to remember that direct discrimination is frequently hidden or covert. Many employers still discriminate against women by

refusing to offer them jobs or promote them, but few employers admit
that this is due to the woman's sex; some other reason will usually be
given. It is the woman who has to prove that she has been discriminated
against, and this is still a difficult task.

Less favourable treatment

'Less favourable treatment' involves some detriment to the person concerned. In *Peake* v. *Automotive Products Ltd* (1978)[5] women were
allowed to leave the factory five minutes before male employees. The
Court of Appeal refused to hold that this was sex discrimination, as the
employer's motive was to prevent the women from being jostled, and it
would be very wrong, according to Lord Denning, if the law was 'to do
away with the chivalry and courtesy which we expect mankind to give to
womankind'. Fortunately, subsequent cases took a rather more robust
approach: in *Ministry of Defence* v. *Jeremiah* (1980)[6] the Court of
Appeal held that it was sex discrimination to stipulate that only men
could work in the 'colour-bursting shell shop' because the women's hair
would be messed up. This counted as less favourable treatment. In *Gill
and Coote* v. *El Vinos Co. Ltd* (1983)[7] it was held to be less favourable
treatment to refuse to serve women at a bar; and in *R.* v. *Birmingham
City Council ex parte EOC* (1989)[8] the loss of a chance of a grammar
school place was held to be less favourable treatment.

On the ground of sex

The second aspect is that the treatment must be on the ground of sex. This
does not mean that the employer *intends* to discriminate; motive is irrelevant. In *James* v. *Eastleigh Borough Council* (1990)[9] a swimming pool
allowed women over the age of 60 free admission, whereas men had to pay
until they reached 65. This was based on the state pension age. The House
of Lords held that this was unlawful sex discrimination. The nature of the
Council's motive was irrelevant: the test for sex discrimination was
whether the men would have been treated differently but for their sex.

In *Hurley* v. *Mustoe* (1981)[10] a woman with three young children was
refused a job because the employer believed that mothers were unreliable
workers. This rule was only applied to women with young children, and
therefore constituted direct discrimination: men with young children
were not in practice excluded. In *Horsey* v. *Dyfed CC* (1982)[11] a woman
was refused secondment for a two-year course in the London area
because her employers believed that, since her husband worked in
London, she would not return to work for them in Wales afterwards.
This would not have been assumed of a married man and therefore constituted sex discrimination. In both these cases, the employers acted on
the basis of stereotyped assumptions, instead of looking at the particular
individuals and their circumstances.

In all cases of direct discrimination, it is necessary to compare a person's treatment with that of someone of the opposite sex. The comparison can be hypothetical; it is not necessary for a woman, say, to show that a man was *in fact* treated more favourably than she was. However, it is necessary to compare like with like. Section 5(3) of the SDA 1975 states that:

> A comparison of the cases of persons of different sex or marital status . . .
> must be such that the relevant circumstances in the one case are the same,
> or not materially different, in the other.

This has caused particular problems in relation to pregnancy, since tribunals initially had some difficulty in imagining the pregnant man. It is also relevant in cases involving dress codes and sexual harassment where parallel situations are generally artificial (see Chapter 4).

Indirect discrimination

Indirect discrimination is defined by section 1(1)(b) as occurring where a person:

> applies to [a woman] a requirement or condition which he applies or
> would apply equally to a man but –
>   (i) which is such that the proportion of women who can comply with
>   it is considerably smaller than the proportion of men who can
>   comply with it, and
>   (ii) which he cannot show to be justifiable irrespective of the sex of
>   the person to whom it is applied, and
> (iii) which is to her detriment because she cannot comply with it.

Similarly, an employer may discriminate indirectly against a married person of either sex on the ground of their marital status.

Indirect discrimination is a concept which enables individuals to challenge seemingly innocent practices, such as requiring certain educational qualifications, or setting age limits, or insisting on physical characteristics, which appear to be neutral but which in fact operate so as to disproportionately exclude one sex. However, unlike direct discrimination, which can never be justified, the employer may be able to show that the practice has some business-related purpose, even though it has an adverse impact on one sex.

The concept of indirect discrimination originated in the US, but the statutory definition in the UK is more specific and limited and has not proved as useful in challenging systematic discrimination. Nevertheless, the law on indirect discrimination is important in combating discriminatory practices in employment, and employers may find it useful to examine recruitment, promotion and training practices to ensure that they do not operate in an indirectly discriminatory manner.

The definition of indirect discrimination contains four distinct elements, and each will be examined in turn.

Requirement or condition
It is necessary to establish that the employer operated a 'requirement or condition'. For example, a stipulation that only full-time employees were eligible for redundancy on a 'last in, first out' basis was a requirement or condition that was indirectly discriminatory to women,[12] as was a requirement that a woman return to work full time after having a baby.[13] It may therefore be unlawful to restrict access to promotion or training programmes to full-time workers.

Similarly, to *insist* that job applicants be under a certain age may be discriminatory, since women are more likely than men to have taken a number of years out of the labour market to care for children. An example is the case of *Price* v. *Civil Service Commission* (1977)[14] where applicants for Executive Officer posts in the Civil Service had to be aged between 17 and 28. If the employer merely *prefers* applicants to be in a certain age group, this will not be unlawful discrimination, even though the preference may exclude all but the most exceptional candidates outside the preferred age range.[15] However, it is clear that tribunals will look at what actually happens, rather than the wording of the job description. In *Jones* v. *University of Manchester* (1993)[16] the employer stated in a job advertisement that the successful applicant would 'preferably' be aged between 27 and 35, but the industrial tribunal nevertheless found that in practice this operated as a requirement. The Equal Opportunities Commission and the Commission for Racial Equality have both argued that the legislation needs to be amended to cover preferences with discriminatory impact. Employers who are serious about equal opportunities should, nevertheless, check such preferences for their impact and ensure that they are justifiable.

Disproportionate effect
The issue of whether a person can comply with a requirement or condition is interpreted broadly. It is not enough that it is theoretically possible for a person to comply – the question is whether they can comply in practice. So in *Price* v. *Civil Service Commission* (1977)[17] the EAT took account of the fact that many women could not apply to the Civil Service between the ages of 17$1/2$ and 28 because of their child-rearing responsibilities.

Comparison of the proportions of men and women who can comply causes certain difficulties. What is the appropriate pool for comparison? What is the relevance and importance of statistics? What does 'considerably smaller' mean? Some useful guidance was given by the Court of Appeal in *Jones* v. *Chief Adjudication Officer* (1990),[18] in which the following approach was advocated:

1. Identify the criteria for selection.
2. Identify the relevant population who satisfy all the other [non-disputed] criteria for selection.
3. Divide the relevant population into groups representing those who satisfy the [disputed] criterion and those who do not.
4. Predict statistically what proportion of each group should consist of women.
5. Ascertain what are the actual male/female balances in the two groups.
6. Compare the actual with the predicted balances.
7. If women are found to be under-represented in the first group and over-represented in the second, it is proved that the criterion is discriminatory.

This approach is particularly helpful in establishing the appropriate 'pool' for comparison. For example, in *Jones* v. *University of Manchester* (1993)[19] the University advertised for a careers adviser, who was a graduate, with relevant experience, and aged between 27 and 35. It was alleged that the age limit amounted to indirect sex discrimination. Under the above approach, the appropriate pool was graduates with relevant experience. The applicant lost her case because she failed to show that the proportion of women graduates with experience who could meet the age requirement was considerably smaller than the proportion of male graduates with experience. She had instead selected a different pool: women who had obtained their degrees as mature students.

It is essential to identify the correct pool, otherwise applicants will find that they do not produce the correct statistical analysis. The use of statistics is itself a difficult issue. Whilst the courts and tribunals have indicated that complex statistical evidence is neither necessary nor desirable, it is obviously important in establishing whether or not indirect discrimination has occurred. Sometimes it will be necessary to produce statistics relating to a particular employer: for example, to demonstrate that a promotion procedure operates in a discriminatory way. Applicants can use the legal procedure of discovery to get the relevant information from the employer. Sometimes the courts are prepared to recognise social realities without detailed statistics, such as that women are more likely to look after young children, and that therefore any requirement for full-time work will exclude more women than men. It is also unclear exactly how great the disparity between the proportion of men and of women who can comply with the requirement or condition must be. In the USA the courts have adopted a 'four-fifths' rule: if the proportion of women who can comply with the requirement is 80 per cent or less of the proportion of men who can comply with the rule, then there is indirect discrimination. The courts in the UK have not adopted this approach: rather, whether or not the respective proportions are 'considerably smaller' is characterised as a question of fact for the Industrial Tribunal, which can lead to divergent results.

The Court of Appeal has given some guidance on this issue in *R.* v. *Secretary of State for Employment ex parte Seymour-Smith and Perez* (1995).[20] After an examination of cases heard by the ECJ the Court of Appeal held that 'before a presumption of indirect discrimination on the ground of sex arises there must be a considerable difference in the number or percentage of one sex in the advantaged or disadvantaged group as against the other sex and not simply a difference which is more than *de minimis*'. But the Court went on to say that the underlying principle is equal treatment, and equal treatment means that 'there shall be no discrimination on gounds of sex'. Accordingly, the Court said, the weight to be attached to the word 'considerable' should not be exaggerated

Detriment

A woman applicant must show not only that she cannot comply with the requirement or condition, but also that this is to her detriment. So it is necessary that there is a real victim of the alleged discrimination. There is little case law on the meaning of detriment, but obvious examples are when someone fails to get a job or a promotion because of the discriminatory requirement or condition. In *De Souza* v. *Automobile Association* (1986)[21] Lord Justice May stated that detriment occurs when:

> the putative reasonable employee could justifiably complain about his or her working conditions or environment, whether or not these were so bad as to constitute dismissal or even if the employee is prepared to work on and put up with the situation.

Justification

Even if a woman can show that there is a discriminatory requirement or condition which operates to her detriment, the employer may be able to justify the existence of such a requirement. What exactly is meant by this? The courts have followed the approach laid down by the ECJ in *Bilka-Kaufhaus GmbH* v. *Weber von Hartz* (1986)[22] that, in order to be justified, measures taken by the employer 'must correspond to a real need on the part of the undertaking, [must be] appropriate with a view to achieving the objectives pursued and [must be] necessary to that end'. This standard was adopted by the House of Lords in *Rainey* v. *Greater Glasgow Health Board* (1987),[23] an Equal Pay Act case, in which the court indicated that the same test should be adopted for the defence of justification in sex discrimination cases. The employer will therefore need to show objective business-related reasons for setting a particular requirement or condition. The tribunals will also balance the discriminatory effect of the requirement or condition against the business advantages to the employer, and it may be relevant that there are other ways of achieving the employer's objective which do not have a discriminatory effect. Nevertheless, tribunals are often willing to accept that certain practices are justifiable without requiring the employer to demonstrate some objective business-related need. For example, seniority as a criterion for redundancy selection was held in *Brook* v. *London Borough of Haringey* (1992)[24] to be self-evidently sensible, without inquiring further into what the employer hoped to achieve. In contrast to this, in *Nimz*[25] the ECJ refused to accept seniority as justifying pay differentials without objective evidence as to the business need that was satisfied. It may be that, in future, tribunals will take a stricter approach to the use of seniority as a criterion.

The exclusion of part-timers from promotion, pension schemes and other benefits generally discriminates against women, and the key issue is frequently whether employers can justify such an exclusion. In *Home Office* v. *Holmes* (1984)[26] the refusal by the employer to allow a Probation Officer to work part time after maternity leave was held to be unlawful discrimination because the employer could not justify the requirement that she work full time. However, in other, similar cases the employer has been able to show a real business need why the job be done full time.

In *Meade-Hill* v. *British Council* (1995)[27] the Court of Appeal held that the inclusion of a nationwide mobility clause in the contract of employment of a married woman was potential indirect sex discrimination. The Court accepted that a higher proportion of women than men are secondary earners, and so a higher proportion of women than men would find it impossible in practice to comply with a direction from their employer to move to an area which necessitated a change of home. However, the Court warned that this was not 'a great and glorious victory' for Mrs Meade-Hill: the employer would be able to justify the mobility clause if they could show their need to be in a position, if circumstances required at any time in the future, to direct an employee of her grade to work elsewhere in the UK. Even if they could not show this, then the clause could be modified so that compliance would not be required from an employee who was unable to comply with it in practice.

In *R.* v. *Secretary of State for Employment ex parte Equal Opportunities Commission*[28] (1994) the Government argued that the exclusion of part-timers from certain statutory rights was justified on the grounds that it created more job opportunities for part-timers. Although increasing job opportunities for part-timers was a legitimate social policy, the House of Lords refused to accept that the means chosen (denying part-timers redundancy and unfair dismissal rights) was either suitable or requisite for achieving that policy.

Other factors, such as age limits, educational qualifications and physical ability, may or may not be justifiable, depending upon the nature of the job.

Remedies under the Sex Discrimination Act 1975

If a tribunal finds that an employer is liable for sex discrimination, then it can make a declaration to that effect. It can also make a recommendation that the employer should, within a specified period of time, take certain steps that the tribunal deems practicable, in order to obviate or reduce the adverse effect of the discriminatory act. So, for example, a tribunal might recommend that an employer meet with representatives of the Equal Opportunities Commission with a view to reviewing and revising its personnel procedures, or that a company change its recruitment procedures. But the tribunal cannot recommend that the employer give the job or promotion, or even the next available vacancy, to the person discriminated against; this would itself be discriminatory.

Tribunals can also award compensation. This is of increasing significance following the decision of the ECJ in *Marshall* v. *Southampton and South-West Hampshire Area Health Authority (No. 2)*[29] that the statutory limit of £11,000 on compensation was contrary to EC law. Following this decision, the government removed the statutory maximum for sex discrimination compensation in the Sex Discrimination and Equal Pay (Remedies) Regulations 1993. Tribunals can now award whatever compensation is considered necessary to compensate the individual who has been discriminated against. This means that sex discrimination could be very expensive for the employer. Tribunals have already made awards in excess of £100,000. These awards cover more than just financial loss: tribunals now regularly award damages for injury to feelings. In *Harvey* v. *Institute of the Motor Industry (No. 2)* (1995)[30] the EAT held that the Regulations had retrospective effect, so that where a tribunal applies an award of compensation after 22 November 1993 (the date the Regulations came into force) there is no limit to the compensation that may be awarded, even though the act of discrimination occurred before the ceiling was lifted.

However, compensation is not awarded in cases of indirect discrimination if the employer can prove that they did not intend to discriminate on the ground of sex. This is being challenged under European law.

The government has also removed the maximum compensation limits for race discrimination and religious discrimination (in Northern Ireland) as well.

Key points

- The SDA 1975 covers non-contractual discrimination and the EqPA 1970 covers contractual discrimination.
- Direct discrimination is defined as less favourable treatment on the grounds of sex or marital status.

- Indirect discrimination occurs when an employer applies a seemingly neutral condition which has a disproportionately adverse impact on one sex and which the employer cannot justify.
- There is no maximum compensation limit. Discrimination can be expensive!

References

1 Bridge L.J. in *Shields* v. *E. Coomes (Holdings) Ltd* [1978] ICR 1159 CA
2 *Legislating for Change*, EOC 1988
3 *The Times*, 4 March 1994
4 *The Times*, 13 June 1995
5 [1978] QB 233
6 [1980] QB 87
7 [1983] QB 425
8 [1989] 2 WLR 520
9 [1990] IRLR 288
10 [1981] IRLR 208
11 [1982] IRLR 395
12 *Clarke* v. *Eley (IMI) Kynoch Ltd* [1983] ICR 165
13 *Home Office* v. *Holmes* [1984] ICR 678
14 [1977] 1 WLR 1417
15 *Perera* v. *Civil Service Commission (No. 2)* [1983] ICR 428
16 [1993] IRLR 218
17 [1977] 1 WLR 1417
18 [1990] IRLR 533
19 [1993] IRLR 218
20 [1995] IRLR 464
21 [1986] IRLR 103
22 [1986] IRLR 317
23 [1987] IRLR 26
24 [1992] IRLR 478
25 *Nimz* v. *Freie und Hansestadt Hamburg* [1991] IRLR 222
26 [1984] IRLR 299
27 [1995] IRLR 478
28 *The Times*, 4 March 1994
29 [1993] IRLR 445
30 [1995] IRLR 416

Chapter 3
Sex discrimination in recruitment

Section 6(1) of the Sex Discrimination Act 1975 (SDA) outlaws discrimination at all stages of the employment process, from recruitment to dismissal. The section states that it is unlawful for an employer to discriminate against a person:

(a) in the arrangements he makes for the purpose of determining who should be offered that employment, or
(b) in the terms on which he offers . . . that employment, or
(c) by refusing or deliberately omitting to offer . . . that employment.

Section 6(2) provides that it is unlawful for an employer to discriminate against a person:

(a) in the way he affords . . . access to opportunities for promotion, transfer or training, or to any other benefits, facilities or services, or by refusing or deliberately omitting to afford . . . access to them, or
(b) by dismissing . . . or subjecting [that person] to any other detriment.

The SDA 1975 makes it unlawful to discriminate 'in relation to employment'. This is defined more widely than for other employment protection legislation and includes employment under a contract of service, apprentices, and 'a contract personally to execute any work or labour'. So it is unlawful to discriminate with regard to independent contractors or self-employed people. However, there has to be a contractual relationship between the parties, and the dominant purpose of the contract must be that the party contracting to provide the services performs the work or labour personally. So in *Mirror Group Newspapers* v. *Gunning* (1986)[1] a contract between the *Daily Mirror* and an independent wholesale newspaper distributor fell outside the scope of the Act.

Temporary workers employed through an agency are covered, both in relation to discrimination by the employment agency (the actual employer) and also as regards discriminatory treatment by the 'principal' – the person for whom the 'temp' is actually working. In *BP Chemicals Ltd* v. *Gillick and Roevin Management Services Ltd* (1995)[2] the EAT held that s. 9 of the SDA was wide enough to cover sex discrimination against agency workers who are not actually working for the principal.

Here Ms Gillick was able to bring an action where the principal, BP, refused to allow her to return to work for them following a period of time off to have a baby. S. 9 will also cover principals who discriminate in the selection of agency staff. Employers who provide training are also covered under the Act, as they have been designated as vocational training bodies.

The government has also finally extended the SDA to cover the armed forces from 1 February 1995. A discriminatory act will not however be unlawful if it is done 'for the purpose of ensuring the combat effectiveness of the armed services'.

The employment must be 'at an establishment in Great Britain', and so excludes contracts where the work is done wholly or mainly abroad. Work on ships, aircraft or hovercraft is covered as follows:

- If the craft is registered in Great Britain, the Act applies unless the work is done *wholly* outside Great Britain.
- If the craft is registered abroad, then the Act applies unless the work is done *wholly or mainly* outside Great Britain.

The Act also covers offshore employment.

Recruitment

As mentioned above, an employer must not discriminate 'in the arrangements he makes for the purpose of determining who should be offered employment'. This is a very wide provision, covering all aspects of the recruitment process, and outlaws both direct and indirect sex discrimination. It is essential for any employer who takes equal opportunities seriously to examine their recruitment process to ensure that it operates in a non-discriminatory way. The Codes of Practice issued by the Equal Opportunities Commission (EOC) and the Commission for Racial Equality (CRE) provide useful guidance on good practice in the area of recruitment. They are also admissible as evidence in any legal proceedings under the Sex Discrimination Act 1975 and the Race Relations Act 1976 (RRA), and any relevant provisions in the Codes of Practice must be taken into account by a tribunal. The Northern Ireland Equal Opportunities Commission has issued a Code of Practice under the Sex Discrimination (Northern Ireland) Order 1976 which provides guidance on removing sex bias from recruitment and selection procedures.

Advertisements

Advertising job vacancies is an important step in ending discrimination.

Informal recruitment methods, whereby jobs are offered to individuals without being widely advertised, tend to have a discriminatory impact. Word-of-mouth recruitment also tends to reproduce the existing race and sex balance of the workforce, reinforcing stereotypes and assumptions about the sort of person who can do the job in question. Advertising vacancies only internally within the organisation has a similar effect, as does advertising at the factory gate. Relying on unsolicited letters of application can also have a discriminatory impact, as can the use of headhunters. Open advertisements are therefore a much better way of ensuring that a wider range of people apply for jobs, but it is essential that the employer considers carefully how and where such advertisements are placed, as well as the content.

In limited circumstances, an employer can indicate in the advertisement that applications are encouraged from a particular sex or racial group. Under sections 47 and 48 of the SDA 1975 and section 38 of the RRA 1976, such encouragement is permissible if it reasonably appears to the employer that there were no or comparatively few people of that racial group or sex doing the work in question in Great Britain, or within a given area, within the last 12 months. However, although an employer can encourage applications, they cannot select a person for interview, or offer them a job, on the basis of their sex or race; such 'positive' discrimination is unlawful.

Section 38 makes it unlawful 'to publish or cause to be published an advertisement which indicates, or might reasonably be understood as indicating, an intention by a person to do any act which is or might be unlawful' under the Act, unless the job is one where sex is a 'genuine occupational qualification' (see below). Using job descriptions with a gender connotation, such as 'waiter', 'salesgirl' or 'postman', is taken as indicating an intention to discriminate, unless the advertisement contains an indication to the contrary. Advertisements are defined widely as including 'every form of advertisement' whether to the public or not. So notices on a company notice-board, internal memoranda, or cards in a shop window are all covered. Care should also be taken with the wording of any job description contained in the advertisement. In *EOC* v. *Eldridge McFarlane-Watts* (1990)[3] a firm of solicitors advertised for a secretary. The advertisement was headed 'The Secretary's Prayer' and continued, 'Let her be willing to listen to her master's voice on eternal tapes and to provide him with endless cups of coffee'. The tribunal found that this gave a clear indication of an intention to discriminate against men. Any illustrations or photographs should also be checked to ensure that they do not give a stereotyped view of the kind of person who does the job.

Advertisements should be placed in publications likely to be read by both men and women, and any recruitment done through schools should ensure that both girls and boys are reached. The EOC Code of Practice recommends that when employers notify vacancies to mixed schools, or the careers service, they should specifically state that the vacancies are open to both sexes.

Section 72 of the SDA 1975 gives the EOC the exclusive right to bring proceedings in respect of discriminatory advertisements, but individuals will also be able to bring tribunal cases on the ground that a discriminatory advertisement is an 'arrangement' under section 6(1)(a).

Selection procedures

A non-discriminatory selection procedure aims to recruit the best person for the job, regardless of any assumptions as to what sort of person that will be. It is therefore important to have a job description, and person specification, that can be used to ensure that discriminatory assumptions are excluded from the selection process. The job description should set out the various elements of the job as done in practice. Whenever a job is re-advertised, the job description should be checked to ensure its continued accuracy.

Particular problems arise with the person specification, since employers tend to have fixed ideas about the right kind of person for the job. These may be vague, such as 'attitude', or specific, such as a particular age limit. It is therefore preferable for a person specification to be drawn up in explicit terms, as this concentrates the employer's mind on exactly what sort of person they want for the job and can help them to realise that certain requirements may have a discriminatory impact. It is much better, for example, that employers specifically address the issue of an age limit, and can justify any such limit, than that they operate under a vague and frequently hidden selection criterion. Similarly, any mobility requirements should be carefully examined: are they really necessary; how often are they exercised in practice? Educational qualifications, particularly when linked with an age limit, may have a discriminatory impact and should be carefully checked to ensure that they really are necessary for the job. A requirement for recent experience may also exclude women applicants and should be checked to see if it really is necessary.

The application form should be examined to ensure that it does not ask candidates for information which is irrelevant to the job, or which could be used consciously or unconsciously to eliminate certain types of candidate. For the majority of jobs it does not matter whether the applicant is married, or has children, or how old any children are, and so such questions should not be included on the application form. If employers do not know whether a woman has children, they cannot discriminate on that basis. Although such information is important for monitoring recruitment policies, it can be recorded on a separate form, together with a statement that it will not be used in the selection procedure.

The EOC Code of Practice recommends that all employees involved in recruitment should be trained in the provisions of the SDA, and the avoidance of unlawful discrimination.

Interviews

It is not unlawful to ask questions at interview about personal circumstances such as marital status or childcare arrangements. However, questions of this nature may be taken as evidence of a discriminatory attitude, and the better approach is to avoid asking such questions unless they are strictly relevant to the job. The EOC Code of Practice suggests that when it is necessary to ask such questions, for example when the job involves unsocial hours or extensive travel, then 'this should be discussed objectively without detailed questions based on assumptions about marital status, children and domestic obligations. Questions about marriage plans or family intentions should not be asked, as they could be construed as showing bias against women.' Nevertheless, research shows that employers frequently ask about family status. Employers who do feel it necessary to ask such questions should ensure that they are asked of both male and female applicants – and should guard against the tendency to construe the answers differently, with men with family responsibilities being viewed more favourably, and women with family responsibilities less favourably.

Tribunals have taken a broad view of what relates to the job in question. In *Saunders* v. *Richmond on Thames Borough Council* (1981)[4] asking a woman golf professional how she thought men would cope with being taught by a woman was held to be legitimate, even though a man would not have been asked a similar question. However, the *Saunders* decision was not followed in *Makiya* v. *London Borough of Haringey* (1990)[5] where a woman who applied for a job as design and technology adviser was asked how she would deal with reactionary male teachers. This was held to be sex discrimination, as none of the male candidates were asked a similar question. *Saunders* was distinguished on the ground that in 1977 asking such a question of a woman golf professional might be seen as 'sensible and practicable', but in 1989 it was impermissible for a self-styled 'Equal Opportunities Employer' to ask such a question only of female applicants.

The EOC Code of Practice states that all those involved in interviews should be trained in the avoidance of unlawful discrimination. Ideally, interviews should be conducted by a panel, rather than a single individual, although this does not necessarily prevent discriminatory questioning. The presence of both men and women on interview panels is also useful in limiting questioning based on outdated stereotypes, but does not, of itself, ensure that such questions are not asked. There is no substitute for adequate training.

It is also recommended by the Code of Practice that records are kept during interviews. Not only is it an important and useful exercise for interviewers to reduce to writing their reasons for rejecting a particular candidate, but such a record will also be necessary in case of any later legal challenge. Indeed, tribunals have shown an increased willingness to infer discriminatory conduct from the employer's failure to keep records. In proceedings under the SDA and the RRA, applicants can use the questionnaire procedure, whereby they ask the employer what the reasons were for their rejection. Failure to answer, or an inadequate answer, can give rise to an inference of discrimination.

Similar considerations apply to interviews for promotion. In *Riches* v. *Express Dairy Ltd* (1992)[6] a part-time woman employee applied for a full-time supervisor's post. At the interview she was questioned about her childcare arrangements and asked how she proposed to manage when her children were ill. She did not get the promotion. The industrial tribunal held that these were questions that arose 'from the assumption, which is still prevalent in many circles, that women tend to take time off to look after children and are therefore less reliable when it comes to timekeeping'.

Tests

Where selection tests are used as part of the recruitment process, employers should take care that the tests themselves are not discriminatory. The EOC Code of Practice states that selection tests 'should be specifically related to job and/or career requirements and should measure an individual's actual or inherent ability to do or train for the work or career'. They should also be reviewed regularly to ensure that they remain free from any bias.

Discriminatory terms of employment

It is unlawful under section 6(1)(b) of the SDA 1975 to offer discriminatory terms of employment. However, if the term relates to the payment of money, the situation becomes slightly more complicated. If the term is *not* accepted then, although the case is brought under the SDA, the plaintiff must show that they would have had a case under the Equal Pay Act 1970 (see Chapter 6) – had the term been accepted. If the offer is accepted, then any claim in respect of discriminatory terms and conditions must be brought under the Equal Pay Act 1970. (Under the RRA, discriminatory terms and conditions are outlawed by section 4(2)(a).)

Genuine occupational qualifications

It is permissible to discriminate on ground of sex if being a man (or a woman) is a 'genuine occupational qualification' (GOQ) for the job. However, it is never permissible to discriminate on the ground of marital status. The GOQ defence only applies in relation to recruitment or promotion: it does not apply to offering discriminatory terms of employment or to dismissal. However, in *Timex Corporation* v. *Hodgson* (1981)[7] a man was selected for redundancy in contravention of a 'last in, first out' agreement because the company wanted to retain a female supervisor to carry out duties such as refilling sanitary towel machines and dealing with women workers' personal problems. The EAT held that the discriminatory act was not dismissing Mr Hodgson, but failing to offer him the supervisor's job. This was therefore covered by the GOQ defence.

The GOQ defence can only be argued in relation to specific circumstances laid down by section 7 of the SDA 1975. It is not possible for employers to argue that they appointed a woman, or man, in order to get a more 'balanced team', even if this is because of a commitment to equal opportunities. Discrimination on the ground of sex at the point of selection is unlawful, whatever the motive, unless it falls within the GOQ defence. However, even though sex may be a GOQ for a particular job, this does not mean that the employer *must* employ someone of that gender. The Act simply provides that if the employer specifies that only men, say, will be considered for the job, then this will not be unlawful. If the employer wishes to employ a woman to play Hamlet, they may do so!

The employer has the burden of proving that the GOQ defence applies, and if the job is to be publicly advertised then it is likely that the publisher will require a statement that it will not be unlawful to restrict applications to one sex only. The defence applies even if only *some* of the job duties fall within the GOQ; however, the employer will not be able to rely on the defence if:

- they already employ employees of one sex who are capable of carrying out the duties in question, and
- it would be reasonable to require these employees to carry out the duties, and
- the numbers of these employees are sufficient to carry out those duties without undue inconvenience.

So if refilling sanitary towel machines can be carried out by existing female employees without any difficulty, the fact that part of the job involves such duties will not allow the employer to rely on the GOQ defence.

Section 7 contains the following GOQs:

- *Physiology or authenticity.* The GOQ defence applies 'where the essential nature of the job calls for a man for reasons of physiology (excluding physical strength or stamina) or, in dramatic performances or other entertainment, for reasons of authenticity, so that the essential nature of the job would be materially different if carried out by a woman'. So it is lawful to insist that a model for women's clothes be female, or that a Tarzanogram performer be male. Physical strength and stamina are expressly excluded: employers may need people capable of lifting heavy weights for a particular job, but they cannot assume that only men will be able to do so.
- *Decency or privacy.* The defence applies where the job needs to be done by a man, say, to preserve privacy or decency because: 'it is likely to involve physical contact with men in circumstances where they might reasonably object to its being carried out by a woman'. So in *Wylie* v. *Dee & Co. (Menswear) Ltd* (1978)[8] the employer argued that she could not employ a woman as a sales assistant in a menswear shop because the job involved taking inside-leg measurements. However, the tribunal found that, in practice, it would only rarely be necessary to take inside-leg measurements, and in any event the shop employed several male assistants who could do this part of the job. Similarly, in *Etam plc* v. *Rowan* (1989)[9] the GOQ defence did not apply when a man was refused a job as sales assistant in a women's clothes shop on the ground that the customers would not want a man in the changing rooms: going into the changing rooms was only a small part of the job, and the shop employed sufficient female sales assistants to carry out this part of the job without any inconvenience.

  The defence also applies if 'the holder of the job is likely to do his work in circumstances where men might reasonably object to the presence of a woman because they are in a state of undress or are using sanitary facilities' and the job therefore needs to be held by a man to preserve privacy or decency. So it may be justifiable to insist that a cleaner of men's toilets be a man, although much will depend upon the circumstances, such as when the toilets are cleaned, whether all or only part of the job involves toilet cleaning, and whether other employees of the appropriate sex are available for that part of the work.

Private homes

Originally, all employment in private homes was excluded from the provisions of the SDA 1975 (this is still the case in respect of racial discrimination), but the ECJ ruled in 1984[10] that this did not comply with the Equal Treatment Directive. It is now only a GOQ where:

> the job is likely to involve the holder of the job doing his work, or living, in a private home and needs to be held by a man because objection might reasonably be taken to allowing a woman –
> (i) the degree of physical or social contact with a person living in the home, or
> (ii) the knowledge of intimate details of such a person's life,
> which is likely, because of the nature or circumstances of the job or of the home, to be allowed to, or be available to, the holder of the job.

So in *Neal* v. *Watts* (1989)[11] it was a GOQ that a nanny be female, because part of the nanny's duties was to take the baby from the mother whilst the mother was in the bath.

Living in

Where 'the nature or location of the establishment makes it impracticable for the holder of the job to live elsewhere than in premises provided by the employer', and the premises available are lived in by men and are not equipped with separate sleeping accommodation or sanitary facilities, and it is not reasonable to expect the employer to provide such facilities for women, then sex is a GOQ. This covers premises such as lighthouses and oil rigs, but it is necessary that employees actually live in. In *Sisley* v. *Britannia Security Systems Ltd* (1983)[12] women security guards worked 12-hour shifts and were provided with sleeping and rest facilities, which the women used in their underwear to avoid creasing their uniforms. The employer advertised for a female security guard. The EAT upheld the complaint of a male applicant: the GOQ defence did not apply, as these were not 'live-in' premises.

Often the key question will be whether it was reasonable for the employer to provide separate facilities. This involves tribunals in a difficult balancing act between the discriminatory impact of not providing separate facilities on the one hand, and the expense to the employer on the other. Much will depend on the size and administrative resources of the employer. It is suggested that, in relation to the building of new premises, it is no longer justifiable to provide single-sex accommodation.

Hospitals and prisons

The GOQ defence will apply where:

> the nature of the establishment, or the part of it within which the work is done, requires the job to be held by a man because –

(i) it is, or is part of, a hospital, prison, or other establishment for persons requiring special care, supervision, and attention, and
(ii) those persons are all men (disregarding any women whose presence is exceptional), and
(iii) it is reasonable, having regard to the essential character of the establishment, that the job should not be held by a woman.

It is unclear whether this provision allows all-male prisons and hospitals to insist upon employing only male staff. In *Secretary of State for Scotland* v. *Henley* (1983)[13] the single-sex establishment GOQ did not apply to a job as hall governor in a men's prison, as two women had been appointed as governors in the past, though the EAT assumed that a consistent policy of not appointing women would be lawful.

Nor does this defence apply to all single-sex establishments: the 'inmates' must require 'special care'. So it did not apply to the appointment of a teacher at a girls' preparatory school attached to a convent.[14]

Personal services

The GOQ defence applies where 'the holder of the job provides individuals with personal services promoting their welfare or education, or similar personal services, and those services can most effectively be provided by a man' – or woman.

This covers obvious cases such as working in a rape crisis centre but, in less obvious situations, everything will depend on the particular circumstances. It is essential that the services are personal; this requires some direct contact between the service provider and the person receiving those services. However, it is not necessary for the employer to show that *only* a man, say, could provide the particular services: the question is whether those services can *most effectively* be provided by a man. Again, this involves tribunals in a difficult balancing act. The comparison must be made between people with the necessary qualifications and experience for the job in question. If a qualified person of one sex would provide the services more effectively than a qualified person of the opposite sex, then the GOQ defence is made out.

Working abroad

The GOQ defence applies 'where the job needs to be held by a man because it is likely to involve the performance of duties outside the UK in a country whose laws and customs are such that the duties could not, or could not effectively, be performed by a woman'. So this might apply, for example, to jobs where certain duties were to be performed in a Muslim country, and a woman would not be able to carry out the requisite duties. Where the job involves work done 'wholly or mainly outside

Great Britain' then the provisions of the Act do not apply in any event.

Jobs held by married couples

Being a man (or a woman) is a GOQ where the job is 'one of two to be held by a married couple'. It is not unlawful under UK law to specify that a job be held by a married person; the effect of this provision is that the employer can state which of the two jobs is to be done by the husband, and which by the wife.

Protective legislation

Most of the protective legislation which restricted the scope of women's employment has been repealed. The SDA 1986 removed the restrictions on women working nights and shift work, and other limitations on hours. Section 51 of the SDA 1975 originally allowed employers to rely on pre-1975 legislation as a defence to a sex discrimination claim, but in *Johnston* v. *Chief Constable of the Royal Ulster Constabulary* (1986)[15] the ECJ held that this general exemption was too wide: the Equal Treatment Directive provides that the principle of equal treatment for men and women should not override provisions concerned with the protection of women, particularly as regards maternity and pregnancy, but the Court ruled that this was to be interpreted narrowly. In the *Johnston* case it did not allow the RUC to refuse to arm women police officers.

As a result of this decision, the Employment Act 1989 was passed. Section 1 provides that any legislation predating the SDA 1975 will be void insofar as it requires an employer to discriminate either directly or indirectly. Where the discrimination is indirect, such as a height requirement, then it will be lawful only if it is justifiable, and the burden of proving justification is placed on the employer. However, employers will still have a defence to an allegation of sex discrimination if they can show that it was necessary to discriminate in order to comply with provisions under the Health and Safety at Work etc. Act 1974, concerning the protection of women as regards pregnancy or maternity or 'other circumstances giving rise to risks specifically affecting women'. This is much narrower than the previous provision, but still allows an employer to argue that discrimination is justified in order to protect women from specific risks. In *Page* v. *Freight Hire (Tank Haulage) Ltd* (1981)[16] a woman tanker driver was not allowed to drive a tanker containing a chemical that was potentially dangerous to women of childbearing age. She told her employers that she did not want children, that she knew of the risks, and that she was prepared to take those risks. Nevertheless, the EAT found that the company was not liable: they had a duty to ensure the health and safety of their employees as far as was reasonably possible, and it was not necessary for them to show that there were other, less discriminatory, ways of avoiding the risk.

However, employers may feel that it is appropriate to look at other means of protecting women in relation to pregnancy, childbirth and reproductive hazards, and to take into account the size of the risk, on the one hand, and the discriminatory effect of the restriction, on the other. Following the *Johnston* decision, it may no longer be justifiable to remove a woman from a job on the basis of a very slight risk to her reproductive capacity.

Using employment agencies and recruitment services

It is unlawful, under section 15 of the SDA 1975, for employment agencies to discriminate against one sex:

- in the terms on which they offer to provide services
- by refusing or deliberately omitting to provide services
- in the way they provide services.

Employment agencies are widely defined as 'a person who, for profit or not, provides services for the purposes of finding employment for workers or supplying employers with workers'. They include Government agencies, such as Job Centres, as well as private employment agencies. In addition, section 15(2) makes it unlawful for a local education authority or education authority to do any discriminatory act in the performance of its training functions. The provision of services includes guidance on careers. Schools' careers services are therefore covered. As a result of section 15, it is unlawful for an employment agency to refuse to send women for interviews for particular jobs, or with particular employers, unless sex is a GOQ.

It is also unlawful for employers to instruct employment agencies to discriminate, or to put pressure on agencies to discriminate. So in *EOC* v. *Precision Manufacturing Services* (1991)[17] it was unlawful for an employer to instruct a Job Centre not to send him males or Muslims for a vacancy for a general operative.

Key points

- Check all recruitment arrangements for potential direct or indirect discrimination.
- Advertise publicly in publications and fora which will reach both sexes.

- Consider encouraging applications from one sex, if previously under-represented.
- Avoid the use of sexist job titles or job descriptions.
- Check the job description and person specification to ensure they are up to date and relevant.
- Check application forms to ensure they do not ask applicants for irrelevant information.
- Provide training in equal opportunities for anyone involved in selection and recruitment.
- At an interview, only ask questions about personal circumstances if they are relevant to the job and ensure any such questions are asked of both male and female applicants.
- Keep records, with reasons, of decisions taken at interviews.
- Ensure selection tests are not directly or indirectly discriminatory.
- If it is possible that a job is covered by a GOQ defence, check this carefully to ensure that the job genuinely falls within one of the categories and consider whether, in any event, it is really necessary to recruit a member of one particular sex.
- Ensure that any employment agency, careers service or Job Centre knows that you are genuinely committed to equal opportunities and that you are seeking the best person for the job.

References

1 [1986] IRLR 27
2 [1995] IRLR 128
3 IT, unreported, 1990, see IRLIB 467, p. 6
4 [1981] ICR 75
5 Unreported, 8.2.90 COIT, see IRLIB 467, p. 9
6 Unreported, IT Case No. 8571/92, see EOR-DCLD No. 15, p. 6
7 [1981] IRLR 530
8 [1978] IRLR 103
9 [1989] IRLR 150
10 *Commission of the European Communities* v. *United Kingdom* [1984] IRLR 29
11 Unreported, 1989, see IRLB 476, p. 6
12 [1983] ICR 628
13 Unreported, EAT, see R. TOWNSHEND-SMITH, *Sex Discrimination in Employment*, 1989, Sweet and Maxwell, London
14 *Fanders* v. *St Mary's Convent Preparatory School*. Unreported, 23.11.89, see IRLB 476, p. 8
15 [1986] IRLR 263
16 [1981] IRLR 13
17 Unreported, see EOR-DCLD No. 12

Chapter 4
Sex discrimination in employment

The Sex Discrimination Act 1975 (SDA) covers all aspects of discrimination against women during employment, except discriminatory contractual terms, which are covered by the Equal Pay Act 1970 (EqPA).

Promotion

Promotion raises similar issues to initial recruitment, and many of the points made in Chapter 3 are relevant here. In particular, it is essential that opportunities for promotion are advertised both internally and externally, if this is appropriate. Problems will almost certainly arise if employers fill promotion opportunities solely on the basis of informal selection: this is an inherently subjective procedure which tends to reinforce existing sex ratios and exclude women from more senior jobs. In *Schofield* v. *Double Two Ltd* (1992)[1] a clothing manufacturer employed two trainee supervisors, one male and one female. The male trainee was offered the post of assistant manager, with the intention that he take over the manager's job at a later date. The post was never advertised and the female trainee was not informed of the vacancy. Ms Schofield, the female trainee, successfully complained of sex discrimination.

A claim of discrimination is far less likely if promotion opportunities are advertised as open to all suitably qualified applicants. Formal procedures also reduce the chance of discrimination. As in recruitment, job descriptions and person specifications should be rigorously checked to ensure that all the key elements are really necessary. In particular, requirements as to length of service and experience can have an indirectly discriminatory effect, and employers should consider whether there are other, less discriminatory ways of achieving the same result.

The EOC Code of Practice gives some guidance on the operation of appraisal systems and promotion procedures and suggests that employers should regularly review promotion and career development patterns to avoid any unlawful indirect discrimination. Tribunals increasingly refer to the Code of Practice in their decisions: one of the main reasons for finding unlawful discrimination in the *Schofield* case was that the employer had not paid any regard to the Code of Practice and in particular paragraph 25(d), which states that 'when general ability and personal

qualities are the main requirements for promotion to a post, care should
be taken to consider favourably candidates of both sexes with differing
career patterns and general experience'. In this case, it was difficult for
women to be promoted to supervisory positions because certain key
technical aspects of the job, such as the operation of cutting room
machines, had traditionally been done by men, and women were unable
to gain the necessary experience. The tribunal concluded that the
employer should have considered the 'justifiable' requirements for the
post very carefully, and at the very least Ms Schofield should have been
told of the vacancy and given the opportunity to apply for it.

The case also highlights the fact that equal opportunities is a continuing process. It may well have been the case that, even if Ms Schofield
had applied, she would not have been appointed because of her lack of
cutting room experience, and that it was justifiable for the employer to
require assistant managers to have such experience. The real problem is
that, in a sex-segregated job market, women still do not have access to
the same range of jobs as men, and this hampers them in gaining promotion. Many organisations have quite rigid demarcations whereby applicants for promotion to senior posts will only be sought from certain
sections of the workforce. Any such practices should be carefully examined for indirect discrimination. The employer may find that, even
though there is a discriminatory impact on women, the restriction is still
justifiable in terms of business need. But even where this is the case,
employers should go on to see whether it would be possible, through
training and other forms of encouragement, to enable women to gain the
relevant experience or qualifications.

Training

Training is a key element of equal opportunities. The SDA 1975 makes it
unlawful to discriminate in the way an employer affords access to training, which is defined as including any form of education or instruction.
The EOC Code recommends that all policies and practices covering
selection for training, day release and personal development should be
checked to ensure that they are not directly or indirectly discriminatory,
and if more men than women are receiving training, then employers should
identify the cause of this to ensure that it is not due to discrimination.

Steps such as examining patterns of training and encouraging women
to take advantage of training opportunities are a form of positive action.
Training is also one of the few circumstances in which the SDA permits
positive discrimination – i.e. treating women differently (and more
favourably) than men. An employer is permitted, under section 48, to
provide only women with access to training facilities to fit them for a

particular kind of work, as long as there were no women, or relatively few, doing the work in question within the previous 12 months. Similarly, an employer can give only women access to training for a post of any kind within the organisation, if in the previous 12 months there were no, or comparatively few, women holding such a post. These provisions offer employers great scope for encouraging women to put themselves in a position whereby they can realistically apply for previously male-dominated jobs. However, employers cannot *guarantee* women those jobs at the end of the training process: only encouragement is allowed. Discrimination at the point of selection is always unlawful.

Dismissal

It is clearly unlawful to dismiss a woman simply because she is a woman: this would be unlawful sex discrimination under the SDA 1975, and also an unfair dismissal under the Employment Protection (Consolidation) Act 1978 (EP(C)A). It may also be unlawful to select an employee for dismissal using criteria which are indirectly discriminatory. It is particularly important to be aware of this when choosing redundancy selection criteria. Making part-time employees redundant first is a practice which obviously has a disproportionate impact on women and may be difficult for the employer to justify.[2] Similarly, the use of length of service as the criterion for redundancy selection, or even as one of a handful of criteria, may discriminate indirectly against women, as may the use of sickness and absenteeism records. Not only should employers be ready to justify such criteria, but they may also wish to examine whether there are other selection criteria which could be used with less discriminatory impact. In *Brook* v. *London Borough of Haringey* (1992)[3] the Local Authority began a redundancy exercise, agreeing criteria with the unions which placed considerable weight on length of service and sickness records. Special exemptions from selection were provided for apprentices, but no such exception was made for older women who had been recruited under a special 'Returners' scheme. Even though the tribunal found that these criteria were, in fact, justifiable and thus not unlawful, the Local Authority effectively wiped out the equal opportunities efforts of previous years.

In *The Post Office* v. *Adekeye* (1995),[4] a case concerning identically worded provisions of the Race Relations Act 1976, the EAT held that Miss Adekeye could not bring a claim of unlawful discrimination in respect of her employers rejecting an appeal against summary dismissal. She had been dismissed, and was appealing for reinstatement. She was not an 'employee' or 'a person employed' at the date of her appeal hearing, as her contract of employment was terminated when she was dismissed. Nor was she alleging any discrimination in the original dismissal. The EAT indicated that they felt this was an unfortunate gap in the protection provided by the statute.

Retirement

The SDA 1975 originally excluded any discrimination in relation to death or retirement. So it was lawful for an employer to insist that women retire at 60 and men at 65. However, in *Marshall* v. *Southampton and South-West Hampshire Area Health Authority* (1986)[5] the ECJ ruled that this was in breach of the Equal Treatment Directive: men and women could not be subject to different retirement ages. As a result of this decision, the SDA 1986 was passed. This provides that employers can no longer discriminate between men and women in relation to retirement – and this covers not only dismissals, but also: job offers which contain discriminatory retirement terms; access to promotion, transfer or training; and subjecting a woman to any other detriment which results in dismissal or demotion. However, the employer is only prevented from treating similarly situated employees differently. In *Bullock* v. *Alice Ottley School* (1992)[6] the retirement age for domestic staff and teachers was 60, whereas maintenance and ground staff did not have to retire until they reached 65. Mrs Bullock alleged that this amounted to sex discrimination. The Court of Appeal disagreed, holding that the SDA 1986 did not prevent employers from having different retirement ages for different categories of staff. There was no direct discrimination, as a man in the same job would have been treated in the same way. Mrs Bullock also alleged that there was indirect discrimination, since all the maintenance and ground staff were men, whereas the vast majority of domestic and teaching staff were women. The Court of Appeal held that, in order to justify the later retirement age for a predominantly male group of workers, the employer would have to show a real and genuine need. Here, the later retirement age was justified because of the difficulty in recruiting maintenance and ground staff, and the need to retain them for as long as possible.

Detriment

It is unlawful to subject a woman to 'any other detriment'. This covers anything which places an employee 'under a disadvantage',[7] and the courts and tribunals are much less likely nowadays to dismiss complaints as too trivial under the *de minimis* rule. Two issues in particular have arisen: sexual harassment and dress codes.

Sexual harassment

Although not specifically referred to in the legislation, it is clear that sexual harassment is unlawful. In *Strathclyde Regional Council* v. *Porcelli* (1986)[8] a female laboratory technician was subjected to 'a policy of vindictive unpleasantness' by two male laboratory technicians who wanted to persuade her to leave. Part of this campaign involved incidents which clearly contained a level of sexual innuendo amounting to sexual harassment. The EAT held that this was conduct on the ground of her sex, which was to her detriment because as a result of it she felt obliged to request a transfer.

Porcelli was important in establishing that unlawful sexual harassment encompasses more than simply a woman's being dismissed for refusing to have a sexual relationship with her boss. It is now clear that the existence of an unpleasant and intimidating working environment is sufficient detriment to establish a case. If the less favourable treatment is on the ground of sex, then this is unlawful, regardless of the motive for the behaviour. It is also clear from the case law that whether a particular course of conduct amounts to sexual harassment depends upon how that conduct is viewed by the woman at whom it is aimed: comments and behaviour that some women find inoffensive can be highly intimidating to others. Although the measure of whether behaviour amounts to harassment is clearly subjective, this has meant that the harasser can argue that the woman encouraged him through her clothing and manner. In *Wileman* v. *Minilec Engineering Ltd* (1988)[9] the fact that the woman wore 'scanty and provocative' clothing to work was held to be relevant as to whether she suffered any detriment. In *Snowball* v. *Gardner Merchant Ltd* (1988)[10] evidence of the sexual content of the complainant's conversation and her past sexual history was admitted as being relevant to the issue of detriment. In *Donnelly* v. *Watson Grange Ltd* (1992)[11] various remarks and suggestions of a sexual nature had been made to the complainant, but the tribunal found that, although such remarks could amount to sexual harassment if the recipient had made it clear that such remarks were unacceptable and the remarks then continued, in this case the impression was that the applicant had 'freely and willingly' taken part in the conversations.

However, sexual harassment is a very difficult issue for women to deal with, and women frequently put up with comments and behaviour because they are uncertain or frightened of the consequences of complaining. In *Van Den Burghen* v. *Nabarro Nathanson* (1992)[12] Miss Van Den Burghen had her breasts squeezed by a trainee solicitor at a Christmas lunch during which solicitors were presented with chocolate penises by their secretaries. She complained to a senior partner, who later told her that following investigation he considered the matter closed due to lack of witnesses. Miss Van Den Burghen was then 'sent to

Coventry' by her colleagues and three months later was made redundant.
The tribunal found that her dismissal constituted unlawful sex discrimination. The conduct at the Christmas lunch amounted to sexual harassment, and thereafter she had been victimised. The case also highlights
the fact that a key issue in sexual harassment cases is the extent to which
the employer is liable for the behaviour of employees; most sexual
harassment occurs between co-workers, rather than employer and
employee. Section 41(1) of the SDA 1975 provides that:

> Anything done by a person in the course of his employment shall be
> treated . . . as done by his employer as well as by him, whether or not it
> was done with the employer's knowledge or approval.

So in the *Van Den Burghen* case the employer was liable for behaviour
at the Christmas lunch because it was 'an office occasion'. In
Bracebridge Engineering Ltd v. *Darby* (1990)[13] the employer was liable
for a sexual assault committed by a charge hand and the works manager
on a woman factory worker, as the assault occurred in the context of the
two men exercising a supervisory and disciplinary role.

In *Insitu Cleaning* v. *Heads* (1995)[14] the EAT held that one remark,
'Hiya, big tits', was capable of amounting to sex discrimination. They
rejected the employer's argument that the remark was not sex-related, as
a similar remark could have been made to a man: 'a remark by a man
about a woman's breasts cannot sensibly be equated with a remark by a
woman about a bald head or a beard. One is sexual, the other is not.' The
employer also argued that one isolated remark could not be 'unwanted
conduct', because the man did not know that it was unwanted by the
woman until she made this clear. The EAT rejected this: to hold otherwise would be to give men a licence to argue that every act of harassment was different from the first, and that they were just testing to see if
it was unwanted. 'No one other than a person used to indulging in loutish
behaviour could think that the remark made in this case was anything
other than obviously unwanted.' The EAT went on to comment that
employers should adopt separate procedures to deal with complaints of
sexual harassment; that this should include informal first steps aimed at
getting the harassment to stop; and that any complaint should be looked
at from the perspective of the person aggrieved.

In *Stewart* v. *Cleveland Guest (Engineering) Ltd* (1994)[15] the EAT
had to consider whether the display of pin-ups in the workplace
amounted to sex discrimination. The EC Commission Code of Practice
on sexual harassment (see below) includes non-verbal conduct in its definition of sexual harassment, and many sexual harassment policies outlaw
the display of nude pictures of women. But the EAT refused to overturn
a tribunal decision that the display of pictures that Mrs Stewart found
offensive was sex discrimination. The tribunal took the view that pin-ups

were 'sex-neutral': a man might have found the pictures as offensive as Mrs Stewart did, and therefore it was not less favourable treatment on the grounds of her sex. This decision can be criticised for failing to realise that men and women will have very different reactions to pictures of naked women: some men are undoubtedly offended by pin-ups, but do not experience the feelings of degradation and humiliation that many women feel. It is difficult to believe that if the form of harassment had been racist graffiti the tribunal would have concluded that because white people might also be offended by it the graffiti could not amount to race-based discrimination.

The employer may have a defence if he or she can show that:

> he took such steps as were reasonably practicable to prevent the employee from doing that act, or from doing in the course of his employment, acts of that description.

It will be much easier for employers to rely on this defence if they have a comprehensive sexual harassment policy. Recently, tribunals have begun to refer to the European Commission's Code of Practice on measures to combat sexual harassment for guidance in this area, and the EAT stated in *Wadman* v. *Carpenter Farrer Partnership* (1993)[16] that the definition in the Code could be helpful to tribunals. It seems likely that, in future, employers will more easily be able to persuade tribunals that they have taken all reasonable steps to avoid sexual harassment if they have followed the recommendations of the Code of Practice.

The European Commission's Code of Practice

The Code of Practice was issued under the auspices of a Commission Recommendation on the protection of the dignity of women and men at work, with the purpose of giving practical guidance to employers. It has been suggested that a failure to follow the Code's recommendations may lead to tribunals' concluding that an employer has not taken 'such steps as were reasonably practicable' and that, conversely, following the Code should establish a defence.[17]

The Code defines sexual harassment as 'unwanted conduct of a sexual nature or other conduct based on sex affecting the dignity of women and men at work'. This includes unwelcome physical, verbal or non-verbal conduct. The Code specifically refers to conduct creating 'an intimidating, hostile or humiliating working environment', as well as to cases in which a person's response to sexual harassment is used as a basis for a work-related decision. The Code stresses that whether conduct amounts to sexual harassment depends upon whether it is unwanted: 'it is for each individual to determine what behaviour is acceptable to them and what they regard as offensive'. Sexual attention can thus become sexual harassment if it persists beyond the stage where it is made clear that such behaviour is unwanted.

The Code goes on to state that sexual harassment may be unlawful as a breach of the Equal Treatment Directive 76/207 and that it may also constitute a breach of criminal and/or civil law in the Member States. The Code makes the important point that, since sexual harassment is linked with women's status at work, the most effective sexual harassment policy is likely to be one which is an integral part of a general equal opportunities policy. The prime objective of a sexual harassment policy, according to the Code, is 'to change behaviour and attitudes, to seek to ensure the prevention of sexual harassment'.

In order to create a climate at work such that employees know that sexual harassment is taken seriously by the organisation, the Code recommends that employers begin by issuing a clear policy statement 'that sexual harassment will not be permitted or condoned and that employees have a right to complain about it should it occur'. The policy statement should make clear what behaviour is not permitted, place a duty on managers to implement the policy, explain the procedure for complaining about sexual harassment, and give undertakings that any complaints will be taken seriously and that employees will not be victimised in any way for bringing such complaints. The policy must be communicated effectively to all employees, so that victims know who to complain to and potential perpetrators are aware of the consequences of such behaviour. Training for managers and supervisors will be a key element of an effective policy. Sexual harassment should be specifically stated to be a disciplinary offence, with the rules making it clear what conduct is unacceptable and what the range of penalties for such conduct is. It should also be made clear that victimisation or retaliation against a complainant is a disciplinary offence in itself.

The first step in an effective procedure should be informal resolution: harassment will frequently stop if the victim tells the perpetrator that the behaviour is unwanted. This may sometimes be difficult, as the woman may be too shy or embarrassed or concerned with possible consequences to confront the perpetrator directly. In such cases, the Code recommends the victim to seek the support of a friend or counsellor, who could talk to the perpetrator. In any event, employers should designate individuals, with the agreement of the trade union, who can provide advice and support, and assist in formal or informal resolution. Such individuals should be given training and adequate resources.

There should also be a formal complaints procedure. As the usual grievance procedure may not always be suitable, for example when the person to whom the complaint would normally be made is involved in the harassment, the procedure should specify an alternative person. The Code also recommends that employees be given a chance to complain to someone of their own sex. Once a complaint has been made, then it should be dealt with in a similar manner to other grievances: investigation, followed by a hearing. Extra sensitivity may be needed in sexual harassment cases and, in particular, strict confidentiality should be observed. The Code recommends that both complainant and alleged harasser should have a right to be represented.

If a complaint is upheld, the Code recommends that, where it is necessary to move or relocate an employee, the complainant should be given the choice of moving or having the harasser moved. Where a complaint is not upheld, the Code states that 'consideration should be given to transferring or rescheduling the work of one of the employees concerned rather than requiring them to continue to work together'. This may be difficult in practice, if both parties feel themselves to be aggrieved.

The Code also recommends that trade unions should formulate a sexual harassment policy and that employees should be made aware of their responsibilities in relation to sexual harassment.

According to the Equal Opportunities Commission there has been a large increase in the number of sexual harassment complaints. A clear policy is the best way for an organisation both to prevent sexual harassment from occurring and to ensure that there will be no legal liability for anything that does happen.

Reporting sexual harassment cases
In the past, newspapers have reported sexual harassment cases in tribunals in great detail, sometimes causing considerable embarrassment to the complainant, the alleged harasser, and the employer – particularly when the tribunal concludes that the harassment did not in fact take place. The Trade Union Reform and Employment Rights Act 1993 (TURERA) now gives industrial tribunals a discretionary power to make a 'restricted reporting order' in cases involving allegations of sexual misconduct. This will make it an offence for anyone to publish or broadcast a report that includes anything that could identify anyone making, or affected by, such an allegation. The order will last until the tribunal's decision is promulgated.

Sexual misconduct is widely defined by the TURERA 1993 as 'the commission of a sexual offence, sexual harassment or other adverse conduct . . . related to sex'. Conduct is related to sex 'whether the relationship with sex lies in the character of the conduct or in its having reference to the sex or sexual orientation of the person at whom the conduct is directed'. This definition would cover unfair dismissal cases where an individual has been dismissed or resigned because of homosexuality (or indeed heterosexuality) as well as sexual harassment cases.

In addition, if the case involves an allegation of an indecent assault or serious sexual offence, the industrial tribunal can remove permanently from the decision any information which would identify any person making or affected by the allegations. Similar powers are available to the

EAT in appeals in cases involving sexual misconduct, including an appeal about an industrial tribunal's decision on whether or not to make a restricted reporting order.

Dress codes

Many employers operate formal or informal dress codes, and these are frequently different in relation to men and women. Employees may argue that having to abide by the dress code is in itself a detriment, or more frequently an employee's failure to follow a dress code may result in disciplinary action being taken against them, up to and including dismissal.

Where an employer's dress code is identical for both sexes, such as a requirement that all employees wear white coats, or green overalls, or are neat and tidy, then no direct sex discrimination can arise. However, more commonly employers apply different rules to men and women. In *Schmidt* v. *Austicks Bookshops Ltd* (1978)[18] the employer required all female employees to wear skirts and overalls. Ms Schmidt was dismissed for refusing to abide by the rule. The EAT held that there was no sex discrimination, since the employer applied a dress code to both men and women; only the content of the code differed. The men, for example, would not have been allowed to wear T-shirts.

Tribunals have tended to follow the approach laid down in *Austick* and hold that there has been no discrimination where the employer has a dress code which applies to both sexes, albeit differently. However, if only women (or indeed men) are subject to a dress code, then there is direct discrimination. In *Creswell* v. *Follett* (1993)[19] a woman was dismissed for wearing trousers three days running, in breach of the employer's dress code. The industrial tribunal held that this amounted to sex discrimination, as there was no evidence that the employers had a dress code for male employees.

Employees who take action over dress codes may also find that tribunals hold that the matter is so trivial that either it does not amount to a detriment or it is *de minimis*, i.e. too trivial for the law to be concerned with. In *Murphy and Davidson* v. *Stakis Leisure Ltd* (1989)[20] a rule requiring female employees to wear nail varnish and make-up was held not to be a detriment, or in any event was *de minimis*.

However, there are signs that the approach of tribunals may be changing in line with changing attitudes as to what is or is not acceptable. In *McConomy* v. *Croft Inns Ltd* (1992)[21] the Northern Ireland High Court ruled that it was unlawful for a pub to refuse to serve a man wearing a small stud earring, despite having an elaborate dress code. The judge said that, whilst it was necessary to take into account 'certain basic rules of human conduct – such as the ordinary rules of decency' which might require or permit different rules for men and women, he found it difficult to see how it could be said that different rules should apply today to men and woman as regards 'the wearing of personal jewellery or other items of personal adornment'. Nor was he prepared to dismiss the matter as too trivial.

Similarly, in *Rewcastle* v. *Safeway plc* (1989)[22] a male employee was dismissed for refusing to cut his hair. The tribunal held that this was unlawful sex discrimination: the rules relating to hair were different for men and women, and the policy was simply designed to mirror conventional differences between the sexes. In *Smith* v. *Safeway plc* (1995)[23] the EAT held that it was sex discrimination to dismiss a male employee who wore his hair in a pony-tail. The EAT placed much emphasis on the fact that restrictions on hair length, unlike dress, affected the employee outside work, as well as at work, and that this amounted to a detrimental interference with individual choice.

However, even where dress codes are held not to amount to direct sex discrimination, it could be argued that they constitute indirect sex discrimination. The dress code is applied neutrally, i.e. to both men and women, but has considerably more impact on women than on men, in that it is a greater restriction for women not to be able to wear trousers than it is for men not to be able to wear T-shirts. The employer would then be required to show some objective justification, not itself based on sexual stereotypes, as to why women could not wear trousers.

Victimisation

It is also unlawful to discriminate against a person by way of victimisation. This is defined as treating a person less favourably than others in comparable circumstances for any of the following reasons:

- that the person brought proceedings under the SDA or the EqPA
- that the person gave evidence or information in connection with any proceedings under the SDA or EqPA
- that the person had otherwise done anything under or by reference to the SDA or EqPA
- that the person had alleged that the discriminator, or any other person, had committed an act which would amount to a contravention of the SDA or EqPA, whether or not the allegation specifically states that.

It is also unlawful discrimination to treat a person less favourably on the grounds that the discriminator knows that the person intends to do any of those things, or suspects that the person has done or intends to do any of those things.

These provisions have been interpreted in a rather limited way by the tribunals. In particular, it is not enough for an applicant to show that they have been less favourably treated than others: the question is whether they have been less favourably treated than others who had not done the acts in question, and that the reason for the less favourable treatment was that they have done such an act in relation to the sex (or race) discrimination legislation. (Because the SDA 1975 and RRA 1976 are almost identically worded, cases under one Act are used to interpret the provisions of the other.) So in *Aziz* v. *Trinity Street Taxis Ltd* (1988)[24] a taxi driver secretly recorded conversations, with a view to taking proceedings under the Race Relations Act 1976, and the other taxi drivers voted to expel Mr Aziz from their co-operative on the ground that this was a breach of trust. The Court of Appeal held that this was not unlawful discrimination, as the motive was not connected with the legislation; rather, it was because of the breach of trust in making the recordings, regardless of the reason behind the decision to make the recordings.

It is unlawful to discriminate against individuals who allege that there has been unlawful discrimination, even when the allegation turns out to be false, as long as the allegation was made in good faith. So in *Sandhu* v. *HM Customs and Excise* (1993)[25] Mr Sandhu, having brought an unsuccessful racial discrimination case against his employer, later alleged that an unfavourable assessment of him was racially motivated. He had earlier been warned that allegations of racial discrimination unsupported by evidence would be treated as potential disciplinary offences. The disciplinary procedures were implemented, and he was reprimanded and required to forgo an increment for a three-month period. This was held to be unlawful, as Mr Sandhu genuinely believed that he had been discriminated against. The industrial tribunal held that in order to show good faith, an applicant could not simply ignore all the evidence, but that here there was sufficient evidence to justify his belief.

Key points

- The operation of promotion and appraisal systems should be carefully checked for hidden indirect discrimination.
- Employers should examine the possibility of providing women with access to training where they have been under-represented.
- Redundancy selection criteria should be carefully examined to ensure there is no disproportionate impact on women.
- Retirement ages and terms should be the same for all employees in the same category, regardless of sex.
- Employers should introduce and monitor sexual harassment policies,

in accordance with the EC Code of Practice.
- Employers should check that dress codes are justifiable and have the same impact on both men and women.
- Employers must not penalise an employee for taking action under sex discrimination legislation.

References

1 Unreported, IT Case No. 54582/91, see EOR-DCLD No. 16
2 *Clarke* v. *Eley (IMI) Kynoch Ltd* [1983] ICR 165
3 [1992] IRLR 478
4 [1995] IRLR 297
5 [1986] IRLR 40
6 [1992] IRLR 564
7 Brandon L.J. in *Ministry of Defence* v. *Jeremiah* [1980] QB 87
8 [1986] IRLR 134
9 [1988] IRLR 145
10 [1988] ICR 318
11 Unreported, see EOR-DCLD No. 15, p. 4
12 Unreported, see EOR-DCLD No. 15, p. 7
13 [1990] IRLR 3
14 [1995] IRLR 4
15 [1994] IRLR 440
16 [1993] IRLR 374
17 See *Equal Opportunities Report* 41, p. 29
18 [1978] ICR 85
19 Unreported, see EOR-DCLD No. 16, p. 6
20 Unreported, see IRLB 469, p. 10
21 [1992] IRLR 561
22 Unreported, see IRLB 469, p. 11
23 [1995] IRLR 132
24 [1988] IRLR 204
25 Unreported, see EOR-DCLD No. 16, p. 3

Chapter 5
Maternity rights

One of the major difficulties for working women is combining their work with family life. Whilst it is important to recognise that children frequently have two parents, in reality the major burden of coping with the day-to-day care of young children falls on women. Women's position in the workplace is unlikely to improve significantly until employers recognise that many of their workers, men included, have family responsibilities, and employers should consider enabling all their employees to share in the responsibility of caring, not only for young children, but also for sick and elderly family members. Career breaks, compassionate leave, paternity leave, and help (both financial and practical) with childcare responsibilities are all important, but as yet are entirely voluntary. It is only in the limited area of maternity rights that the law lays down any entitlement on behalf of employees. Nevertheless, employers who are genuinely interested in equal opportunities will recognise that, by providing greater rights and facilities than are required by the letter of the law, they enable workers to achieve their full potential and have a greater chance of retaining workers who they may have invested in considerably. This chapter will examine an employer's legal obligations to pregnant women, but it should be remembered that all these rights can be improved on by offering enhanced contractual terms, to fathers as well as mothers.

Statutory maternity rights were introduced in the UK in 1975, but have been improved considerably as a result of the European Council Directive 92/85 on Pregnant Workers. The Directive required Member States to implement its terms by October 1994.

Antenatal care

Section 31A of the Employment Protection (Consolidation) Act 1978 (EP(C)A) was enacted in 1980 as a result of concern over the UK's poor perinatal mortality record and provides that pregnant employees have the right not to be unreasonably refused paid time off in order to receive antenatal care. Antenatal care covers any appointment made on the advice of a doctor, midwife, or health visitor. So it would include relaxation classes, or dental appointments, as well as attending an antenatal clinic. The woman must be pregnant, and she must have an appointment. If her employer requests, she must show confirmation from her doctor, midwife or health visitor that she is pregnant, and an appointment card. However, this does not apply to her first appointment, for obvious reasons.

There is little case law in this area. The right is not to unlimited time off, simply not to be unreasonably refused paid time off – suggesting that there may be a point at which an employer can reasonably refuse time off. However, it seems that employers cannot ask an employee to make up the time off, nor to rearrange her hours or shifts. It may be reasonable to ask an employee to make an appointment at the beginning or end of the day, rather than in the middle, but it is often difficult for an employee to choose the time of her appointment.

The employee is entitled to be paid at 'the appropriate hourly rate', calculated in accordance with her week's pay:

- If her hours are always the *same*, then the appropriate hourly rate is simply the week's pay divided by the normal number of hours worked.
- If the hours *vary*, the rate is the week's pay divided by the average number of hours, calculated over the preceding 12 weeks.
- If the employee has variable hours, but has been working for the employer for less than 12 weeks, then the rate is the week's pay divided by an average of normal working hours, calculated as the average number of hours the employee could expect to work in accordance with her contract and the experience of other comparable employees.

If the employer refuses to give the employee time off, she is not entitled simply to go ahead with the appointment. Instead, her remedy is to complain to an industrial tribunal within three months of the date of the appointment. If the tribunal finds that the employer was unreasonable in refusing her the time off, then she must be awarded compensation equivalent to the amount of pay she would have received had she been allowed the time off. Where an employee takes the time off without permission, the employer is entitled to treat this as an act of misconduct and deal with it under their disciplinary procedure, if this is thought appropriate.

The right to maternity leave

The statutory maternity rights scheme originally created two separate rights: a right to maternity pay, available to women with at least 26

weeks' continuous employment with the same employer; and a right, not
to maternity leave itself, but to return to work, available to women with
at least two years' continuous employment. Following the EC Directive
on Pregnant Workers, the TURERA 1993 has introduced new provisions:

- All women, regardless of length of service, now have a new right to
  maternity leave of up to 14 weeks.
- Women with two years' continuous service at the 11th week before
  the expected week of childbirth will continue to have a right to return
  to work up to 29 weeks after the birth of the child.

There are important differences between the two rights.

The maternity leave period

The TURERA 1993 amends the EP(C)A 1978 so that all women, regardless of length of service, will be entitled to take up to 14 weeks' maternity leave. This is to be known as the maternity leave period (MLP).
While a woman is absent from work during her MLP, she is entitled to
the benefit of all her terms and conditions of employment, as if she was
not absent – with the exception of 'remuneration'. This is an important
change. It is not enough that the contractual terms of a woman on maternity leave are 'frozen' – so that holiday entitlement does not accrue, for
example. Rather the Act requires that, apart from 'remuneration', a
woman must be treated as if she were not absent at all. So she will be
entitled to keep a company car, and her holiday entitlement will continue
to accrue, just as if she were working.

The only exception is 'remuneration', but inevitably there will be
uncertainty as to what exactly 'remuneration' means in this context. The
Government's intention, in accordance with the Directive, is that women
continue to receive all benefits in kind, and only wages or salary are
excluded, with the money that women receive during the MLP to be
dealt with through the Social Security system. But what about a company that allows employees to chose whether they have a company car or
a cash allowance? Does one woman have the right to keep the car, but
another loses her allowance? What about profit sharing, or bonuses? Do
these accrue as if the woman had never been away? How can any profit-
related pay element be measured for an employee who has been absent
for 14 weeks? This provision is certain to give rise to a large number of
tribunal cases in the future, and employers may feel it is safer to err on
the side of caution. The Government brought into force paras. 5 and 6 of
Schedule 5 of the Social Security Act 1989 with effect from 23 June
1994. In future, pension schemes must treat a woman who is on maternity

leave and who is receiving statutory or contractual maternity pay as if she were working normally and receiving the remuneration she would normally receive. This applies in calculating continuity, accrual of rights, and benefits. The employee, on the other hand, can only be required to make contributions based on the amount of maternity pay she actually receives. These provisions also apply if employees are absent for 'family reasons' and are paid any contractual pay.

The MLP begins on the date that a woman has notified to her employer (the 'notified leave date'). This date cannot be earlier than the 11th week before the expected week of childbirth, nor can it be later than the day the baby is actually born. However, if a woman is absent from work wholly or partly because of pregnancy or childbirth after the beginning of the sixth week before the expected week of childbirth, then her MLP is deemed to start on the first day of any such absence. So if, for example, a woman tells her employer that she intends to stop work two weeks before the baby is due, but in fact stops work four weeks before the baby is due because of some pregnancy-related condition, then her MLP starts four weeks before the birth. But if she is off work for pregnancy-related reasons nine weeks before the due date, then she can choose to take this as sick leave and begin her MLP later. Some difficulties may arise where a woman is absent for just a day or two within the six-week period, but then wishes to return to work and not begin her maternity leave until the later original notified date. It will then be up to the employer to decide whether he wishes to insist that her MLP has begun, or to allow her to stick to the original date. If a woman is absent from work because of pregnancy or childbirth within the six-week period, she must notify her employer as soon as is reasonably practicable that she was absent for that reason. A failure to do so could result in her losing her entitlement to maternity leave.

Once begun, the MLP lasts for up to 14 weeks, or until the birth of the child, whichever is later. So if a woman began her maternity leave 11 weeks before the baby was due and the baby was more than three weeks overdue, then her MLP would last until the child was actually born. However, if there are health and safety regulations which, because she has recently given birth, prohibit the mother from working after the end of the MLP, then her MLP will continue until the end of the later period.

There is also provision for a woman who is unable to return to work at the end of the MLP because of illness. It will be automatically unfair to dismiss a woman for a reason connected with her having given birth, if:

- before the end of her MLP she gave her employer a doctor's certificate stating that she would be incapable of work at the end of the MLP; and
- she was dismissed within four weeks of the end of the MLP, whilst she was still covered by the doctor's certificate.

There is no length-of-service requirement, but this is not an extension of the MLP: it is simply an unfair dismissal if a woman is dismissed in these circumstances. An employer is therefore not obliged to continue all contractual benefits during the period covered by the doctor's certificate; it would be lawful to ask for the company car back, for example. The illness does not need to be connected with pregnancy or childbirth, but only an illness of the mother herself is relevant; it would not be automatically unfair to dismiss a woman who could not return because her baby was ill. Employers should be wary of dismissing a woman even after the four-week period is up, or where she does not produce a doctor's certificate, as she may be able to show sex discrimination on the ground that a man in analogous circumstances, such as recovering from an operation, would not have been dismissed. In addition, any employees with two years' continuous employment by the end of their MLP would be able to bring an 'ordinary' unfair dismissal action.

Notice provisions
There are strict notice requirements and failure to give notice will generally result in a woman losing her maternity rights.

- *Notification of pregnancy.* Section 37 of the EP(C)A 1978 (as revised by the TURERA 1993) requires an employee to inform the employer *in writing* at least 21 days before her MLP begins:
    - that she is pregnant, and
    - the expected week of childbirth.
  If the employer requests, the woman must produce a certificate from a doctor or midwife stating the expected week of childbirth. In practice, this will normally be the MAT B1 form, which also satisfies the notice requirement.
- *Notification of the start of MLP.* Section 36 requires an employee to notify her employer of the date when she intends her maternity leave to begin (the 'notified leave date') not less than 21 days before that date, or as soon as is reasonably practicable.
- If an employee is *absent from work 'wholly or partly because of pregnancy and childbirth'* after the beginning of the sixth week before the expected week of childbirth, she must notify her employer as soon as is reasonably practicable that she was absent for that reason.
- Similarly, if *childbirth occurs before the notified date*, or before the woman has notified a date, she must notify her employer as soon as is reasonably practicable that she has had the baby.

Only the notification of pregnancy and the expected week of childbirth need be in writing. However, the employer can require that notice be given in writing, and it is suggested that this should be done in the interests of clarity.

There is an exception to the notice requirements where it is 'not reasonably practicable' for a woman to give notice, but this has been interpreted very strictly by industrial tribunals; an employee who cannot decide whether she wants to return to work, and so fails to give notice, will lose her rights. Ignorance of the law is generally no defence, but employers can ensure that employees know about the notice requirements by providing employees with information about maternity leave procedures, including a relevant timetable.

Failure to comply with any of these notification provisions (unless not reasonably practicable) will result in the woman losing her right to take maternity leave. She may also lose her protection against dismissal. If the employer dismisses her for a reason connected with the pregnancy whilst she is working for them, then that constitutes an unfair dismissal. But if the woman goes on leave without complying with the notice requirements, then she is not regarded in law as being on maternity leave, and the employer can dismiss her without facing an action for an unfair dismissal on the ground of pregnancy. However, where the woman has two years' continuous service, she can bring an 'ordinary' unfair dismissal action.

Employers can waive their rights to notice by contract, or by agreement allow the woman to take maternity leave despite failing to meet the notice requirements. It is important to remember that all maternity rights can be improved by more generous contractual terms. However, notification is important for both sides, and in practice it will be preferable for employers to ensure that all pregnant employees are fully aware of both their rights and their obligations under the maternity leave provisions, and then to deal with individual cases with discretion.

Normally, the MLP will last for 14 weeks. If an employee wishes to return to work earlier, she must give the employer *not less than seven days' notice* of the date on which she intends coming back to work. If the employee comes back to work without notifying the employer in advance, or gives them less than seven days' notice, then the employer is entitled to postpone the return until a date that gives them, in effect, seven days' notice and the employer is under no obligation to pay the woman until the date they specify for return. So where an employer takes on a temporary replacement to cover the woman's absence, the requirement of seven days' notice before the woman's return will enable the employer to give adequate contractual notice to her replacement.

The right to return to work

A woman is entitled to extended maternity leave, in addition to the 14-week maternity leave period, in the following circumstances:

- if she has been continuously employed by the same employer, working *over 16 hours a week*, for *two years* at the 11th week before the expected week of childbirth
- if she has been continuously employed by the same employer, working *between 8 and 16 hours a week*, for *five years* at the 11th week before the expected week of childbirth.

This right is to return to work at any time between the end of her MLP (the first 14 weeks) and the 29th week after the beginning of the week in which childbirth occurs.

The employee must notify the employer *in writing* that she intends to exercise this right at least 21 days before her MLP begins, or as soon as is reasonably practicable. If this notice is not given, then the right is lost, and women are therefore well advised to tell employers that they intend coming back to work, even if they are not sure whether they will do so. However, this can create a problem for employers, as they are unable to engage or train full-time replacements for women who, for a variety of reasons, do not in fact come back to work. In order to alleviate this problem, the EP(C)A 1978 provided that, not earlier than 49 days after the expected week of confinement, an employer could write to the woman asking her to confirm that she still intended to return. Failure provide written confirmation, or failure to reply at all, meant that a woman lost her rights, unless it was not reasonably practicable for her to reply. This provision remains in force, but the TURERA 1993 has changed the timing of the employer's letter. The employer can now request written confirmation 'not earlier than twenty-one days before the end of the maternity leave period'. However, it may make sense for employers to write to employees on maternity leave later rather than sooner: the point is to receive accurate information about the woman's intentions. For example, where a woman begins her MLP at the earliest possible date, i.e. 11 weeks before the expected week of childbirth, the employer can write round about the time that the baby is due (and babies are frequently late.). At this stage, the woman may not have really thought about the practicalities of returning to work, and would be well advised to write back confirming her intention to return, even though she is still undecided. There is therefore little point in writing so early: it would be better to write later, and so get a more realistic reply as to whether the woman intends to return.

If the woman does intend to come back, then she must also give the employer written notice of her intention to return to work at least 21 days before the 'notified day of return'. If she does not do so, she loses her right to return. The right is to return not later than the last day of the 29th week after the beginning of the week in which childbirth *actually occurs*, rather than the expected week of childbirth. The notification rule has been strictly interpreted. In *Lavery* v. *Plessey Telecommunications Ltd* (1982)[1] Miss Lavery gave only five days' notice, whereas under the existing law she was required to give seven days' notice. In fact, she could have given seven days' notice, as her baby had been born on 20 April, rather than 2 April, and so she had an extra 18 days in hand. However, the Court of Appeal ruled that, by not giving seven days' notice, she had lost her right to return.

It is important to realise that the notice requirements can be altered by the contract of employment, and this can be done quite informally. In *Lucas* v. *Norton of London Ltd* (1984)[2] Miss Lucas had a very vague discussion with her employer about the possibility of her returning to work after her baby was born. When she telephoned to say that she was ready to come back she was told that her job no longer existed and was given two weeks' salary in lieu of notice. She had not complied with the statutory requirements, but the EAT held that her contract of employment had been varied so that she was entitled to return to work after a reasonable time and on reasonable notice. She remained employed throughout her period of leave, although she was not obliged to work and her employer was not obliged to pay her. By refusing to let her return, the employer had dismissed her. It is obviously unsatisfactory that something as important as the right to return should depend upon rather vague, orally agreed variations to the contract, and it is suggested that employers should stick to the statutory notice periods, or replace them with clear *written* terms.

Lucas also raises the difficult legal issue of what happens to the contract of employment during maternity leave. It is now clear that during the 14-week MLP the contract continues to exist; however, there has been uncertainty as to what happens during the extended period during which a qualifying employee can exercise the right to return. Is the contract terminated, or suspended, or does it continue? The better view now is that the woman's contract continues, but with varied terms – as in *Lucas*, there is no obligation on the employer to pay, or the employee to work. The importance of this is that, if the employee is dismissed whilst on maternity leave, or if the employer breaks an important term of the contract which justifies the woman in resigning, she may be able to bring an 'ordinary' action for unfair or constructive dismissal. However, if the employee is prevented from returning to work by her employer, she cannot bring a 'special' unfair dismissal case, based on the employer's refusal to let her exercise her right to return, under section 56 of the EP(C)A 1978, unless she has complied with the notice provisions. It is perhaps understandable that judges have criticised the maternity legislation as 'exceeding the worst excesses of tax statutes'.

In *Hilton International Hotels (UK) Ltd* v. *Kaissi* (1994)[3] the EAT confirmed that the contract of employment may continue during maternity

leave, and the fact that the employee fails to comply with the notice procedure does not mean that the employee loses their right not to be
unfairly dismissed. Here, Mrs Kaissi received sick pay from her
employer up to the day her baby was born; she had given no written notification of her intention to return to work. When she did write to her
employer some months later to say that she was too ill to return, they terminated her contract on the grounds that she had failed to give the requisite notice. This was a dismissal, and was unfair, owing to a lack of any
proper investigation. Such dismissals may also be automatically unfair in
accordance with s. 60 EP(C)A 1978, if the illness is connected with
pregnancy or childbirth (see below), and can also be sex discriminatory –
with the potential for unlimited compensation.

Postponing the right to return
The right to return can be postponed in three circumstances.

- The *employer* can postpone the woman's return for any good reason
  for up to four weeks. The woman must be told why her return is being
  postponed, and the date on which she can return.
- The *woman* can postpone the right to return for up to four weeks on
  the ground of ill health. She can either do this before she has given
  notice to return, or she can give notice to return in the ordinary way
  and then postpone. But she cannot extend her leave more than once.
  So if an employee notifies a date later than the 29th week because of
  ill health, she must return on that date, and cannot postpone again on
  the ground of ill health. Similarly, if she originally notified a date
  within the 29 weeks, and then postpones her actual return, she cannot
  postpone again. She must come back to work, or she loses her rights.
  So in *Kelly* v. *Liverpool Maritime Terminals Ltd* (1988)[4] Ms Kelly had
  back trouble towards the end of her 29 weeks and sent the employer a
  letter and sickness certificate. She sent in a further two certificates, and
  the employers wrote to her stating that she would not be able to return.
  The Court of Appeal held that she had lost her right to return. The fact
  that the employers did not respond when she sent in the certificates did
  not mean that they had implicitly accepted that she was now on sick
  leave. Only one postponement was allowed. Employees would therefore be well advised to struggle in to work at the end of their four-
  week extension, even if only for a morning, and then go on sick
  leave!
- If there is an '*interruption of work*' on the date nominated for return,
  then the employee need not return until the interruption has ended 'or
  as soon as is reasonably practicable thereafter'. This is designed to
  cover situations of industrial action or lock-out.

It is possible for all three situations to apply, one after the other. The woman must then return on the latest date. But it may still be unlawful to dismiss women who fail to return at the end of the period: in *McClenaghan and Rice* v. *British Shoe Corporation Ltd* (1993)[5] an industrial tribunal held that it was unlawful sex discrimination to dismiss two women who were unable to return after four weeks because of illness: 'they were entitled to be treated in the same manner as any sick employee with a similar employment history would have been treated.' But for their pregnancies, they would not have been denied access to sick pay or sick leave.

Contractual rights during absence

There are now two distinct periods of maternity leave:

- the MLP of 14 weeks that is available to all women
- the extended period of up to the 29th week after childbirth, for those women who qualify.

During the first 14 weeks, a woman's contractual rights accrue as if she had not been absent. However, during the extended period, employers are only obliged to preserve contractual rights on her return. So holiday entitlement will continue to build up during the first 14 weeks, but after that it need not accrue, as long as when she returns she is not penalised for having been absent. Similar considerations apply to pension rights, healthcare schemes, and other contractual entitlements. However, employers may find that they face sex discrimination claims if women on extended maternity leave are treated less favourably than male employees who have similar time off on the ground of ill health (see below).

Right to return to the job

Where an employee is entitled to only the basic 14-week MLP, she has the right to return to her old job and must be treated as if she had not been absent. If a redundancy situation arises during her MLP, so that it is not reasonable for her employer to continue to employ her under her existing contract, then she must be offered a suitable alternative job, if one is available, either with her employer, their successor, or an associated employer. The new contract must begin when the old one ends, and the job must be one where the work to be done under the new contract is suitable in relation to the employee's status, appropriate for her to do in the circumstances, and on terms and conditions not substantially less favourable than in her previous job. However, if there is no suitable alternative vacancy and the woman is made redundant, she is not entitled to a redundancy payment, as she does not have the necessary two years' continuous service. However, she will of course be entitled to any contractual redundancy payment.

Where an employee is entitled to the extended period of leave, then at the end of this period she is also entitled to return to her old job, on the same, or better contractual terms. Pension rights and holiday rights etc. take up from where they left off. The employee's right is to return to 'the job in which she was employed'; so whilst it would seem that some change in the actual duties performed is permissible, if 'the job' is changed, then the employer is in breach of their obligations. Also, terms and conditions must be no less favourable than they would have been had she not been away. In *McFadden* v. *Greater Glasgow Passenger Transport Executive* (1977)[6] Miss McFadden was employed as a CG3 clerk in the Building Section; when she returned from maternity leave she was made a supernumerary CG3 clerk in the Traffic Department. The tribunal held that this was not the same job and, in any event, her terms and conditions were worse.

What if the employer cannot offer the woman her old job back? The employer's legal liabilities vary according to whether this is due to redundancy or some other reason:

- If the reason is *redundancy*, then the employer must offer her any available suitable vacancy. If the employer has no suitable vacancy, then they must see whether an associated employer has a suitable vacancy and offer it to the woman. If either the employer or an associated employer has such a vacancy, and they fail to offer it to the woman, then this automatically constitutes an unfair dismissal. If no such vacancy exists, then the employee is made redundant and is entitled to a redundancy payment in the ordinary way. The employee may also be able to allege that it was unfair to select her for redundancy and may bring an unfair dismissal claim. If the reason she was selected was connected with pregnancy or maternity leave, then that is automatically an unfair reason.
- If the employer claims that it was not reasonably practicable to offer the woman her old job back for *some other reason*, then the woman can bring an unfair dismissal claim. However, the employer can defeat her claim by showing:
  - that it was not reasonably practicable to give her the old job back (for a reason other than redundancy), and
  - that the employer (or an associated employer) offered her employment which was suitable, appropriate, and on no less favourable terms, and
  - that she accepted or *unreasonably* refused the offer.

There is also an exception for small employers, defined as having five

or fewer employees, including the woman seeking to return. Here, the employer can defeat the woman's unfair dismissal claim by showing:
- that it was not reasonably practicable to allow her to return to work (this can be for any reason, including redundancy), and
- that it was not reasonably practicable for her to be offered suitable alternative employment, either with the original employer or an associated employer.

However, if the reason is redundancy, the woman will still be entitled to a redundancy payment.

Suspension

The TURERA 1993 gives employees important new rights regarding suspension from work. Firstly, an employee is to be treated as suspended on maternity grounds if, on the grounds that she is pregnant, has recently given birth, or is breast feeding, she is suspended from work:

- because of any statutory requirement
- because of any recommendation in any relevant code of practice issued under the Health and Safety at Work etc. Act 1974.

As a result of the EC Pregnant Workers Directive, the Government introduced the Management of Health and Safety at Work (Amendment) Regulations 1994, which came into force on 1 December 1994. The Regulations require employers to assess the risk 'by reason of her condition, to the health and safety of a new or expectant mother, or to that of her baby, from any processes or working conditions, or physical, biological, or chemical agents'. The risks are to be assessed with respect to three categories of workers: pregnant; those who have given birth in the previous six months; and those who are breast-feeding. Where a risk is exposed, then the employer should take whatever preventative action is necessary to avoid the risk. If such action would not avoid the risk, then the employer should change the employee's working conditions or hours. If this would not avoid the risk, then the employer must offer any available suitable alternative work. If this would not avoid the risk, then the employer must suspend the woman on full pay. The only exception to this is where the woman has unreasonably refused the alternative work. In addition, if a new or expectant mother works at night, and produces a medical certificate stating that she should not perform night work, then the employer has to transfer her to daytime work or suspend her with pay.

The Health and Safety Executive has issued formal guidance on how the new Regulations should be applied by employers. Employees have

also been given the right to sue the employer for damages if they have
been injured as a result of their employer's failure to comply with the
Regulations.

Childbirth

The TURERA 1993 does away with the concept of 'confinement'.
Instead, there is a new term – 'childbirth' – and the various rights and
notice provisions are tied to the expected *week of childbirth*. Childbirth
is defined as 'the birth of a living child, or the birth of a child either living or dead after 24 weeks of pregnancy', whereas confinement was
restricted to births after 28 weeks of pregnancy.

Dismissal

The TURERA 1993 made significant changes to the right not to be
unfairly dismissed for pregnancy-related reasons. Originally, section 60
of the EP(C)A 1978 made it automatically unfair to dismiss a woman
because she was pregnant, but only women with two years' continuous
service could bring a claim, and the employer had a defence if the
woman was incapable of adequately doing her job, or if she could not
continue working without contravening health and safety regulations. All
changed when the new section 60 came into force on 19 October 1994. It
is now automatically unfair to dismiss a woman because of pregnancy,
or any related reason, regardless of length of service or hours of work.

The new section 60 states that the following are *automatically unfair*:

- to dismiss a woman where the reason or principal reason is that she is
  pregnant or any other reason connected with her pregnancy
- to end a woman's maternity leave period by dismissal, and the reason
  is that she has given birth to a child or any other reason connected
  with her having given birth to a child
- to dismiss a woman after she has returned to work if the reason or
  principal reason for the dismissal is that she took maternity leave
- to dismiss a woman who provided her employer with a medical certificate stating that she would be incapable of work after the end of her
  maternity leave period, and her dismissal is within four weeks of the
  end of her maternity leave period, and the reason is that she has given
  birth to a child or any other connected reason
- to dismiss a woman who cannot continue working on maternity
  grounds because of health and safety regulations: the woman should
  be offered alternative work, or suspended with pay
- to make a woman redundant whilst she is on maternity leave, unless

she has been offered any suitable alternative employment available.

This provides comprehensive protection against dismissal for all pregnant women. Previously, women who were dismissed with less than two years' service had no rights, unless they could show that the employer had discriminated against them on the grounds of sex. So in *Webb* v. *EMO Air Cargo (UK) Ltd* (1993)[7] a woman was taken on as a temporary replacement for another woman who was going on maternity leave. When the woman informed the employer that she too was pregnant, he dismissed her, as she would be unavailable to work during the period that the first woman would be on maternity leave. The House of Lords held that this was not a breach of the SDA 1975, as the reason she was dismissed was her unavailability to do the job; a man who was similarly unavailable would also have been dismissed. The House of Lords referred the case to the ECJ on a point of European law (see below), but under the new section 60 it seems likely that a dismissal in these circumstances will be automatically unfair, as a dismissal for 'any other reason connected with her pregnancy'. Pregnant women and women on maternity leave clearly form a special protected group who employers dismiss at their peril. It is suggested that employers should take great care to ensure that, when a pregnant woman is dismissed, the reason can be proved to be completely unconnected with their pregnancy. This may well be difficult; poor performance and poor sickness records may frequently be connected with pregnancy, and employers should investigate very carefully. The employer may not always know that the woman is pregnant, but if they dismiss an employee for persistent lateness, for example, without first asking whether or not the woman is pregnant, this will still be a dismissal for a pregnancy-related reason and therefore automatically unfair.

However, where a woman does not have two years' continuous service, she will have the burden of proving that the reason for the dismissal was pregnancy related. In order to assist women, the new law states that whenever a woman is dismissed whilst she is pregnant, or after childbirth where her maternity leave period is ended by dismissal, then the employer must provide her with a written statement of the reasons for her dismissal. This must be done regardless of whether or not the woman asks for written reasons. Nor is there any need for the woman to have two years' continuous employment. The penalty for failing to give written reasons is two weeks' pay.

Pregnancy and sex discrimination

There has been considerable confusion in UK law as to whether a dismissal, or refusal of a job, or other unfavourable treatment at work because of pregnancy is unlawful sex discrimination. Many of the cases arose as a result of employers dismissing pregnant women with less than two years' service. These women could not use the unfair dismissal legislation, so their only possible remedy lay in an action under the SDA 1975. As a result of the changes introduced by the TURERA 1993, any woman dismissed because of pregnancy or a pregnancy-related reason is now able to bring an unfair dismissal claim, regardless of length of service. However, it is still important to establish whether treatment on the grounds of pregnancy is sex discrimination in relation to the recruitment and treatment of employees.

The difficulty with pregnancy is that men do not get pregnant, and the SDA 1975 requires a comparison to be made between how an employer treated the woman and how a man in similar circumstances would have been treated. The approach taken by the UK courts is generally to compare a pregnant woman with a man who would require a similar amount of time off because of illness. So if an employer refuses to give a pregnant woman a job because she would be off work for three months, the relevant comparison is with a man applying for a job who would also require three months off in order to undergo a hernia operation. If the man would have also been refused a job, then there is no sex discrimination. However, UK law has been thrown into some confusion because of two cases in the ECJ. In *Dekker* (1991)[8] a woman applied for a job when she was pregnant and was initially recommended for the post. However, the employers refused to employ her because under Dutch law they would have had to pay her maternity pay, but would have been unable to recover this from their insurers. The ECJ ruled that this was in breach of the Equal Treatment Directive. The treatment was based on pregnancy, and as only women can get pregnant this was direct sex discrimination. There was no need to compare the woman with a hypothetical man.

In *Hertz* v. *Aldi Marked K/S* (1991)[9] a woman returned to work after maternity leave, but due to an illness connected with childbirth she had over 100 days' sick leave in the following year. In accordance with their policy on extended sickness absences, the employers dismissed her. The ECJ ruled that to dismiss a woman because of pregnancy, or whilst on maternity leave was direct sex discrimination in breach of the Directive, but that once a woman returned from maternity leave she was only entitled to be treated in the same way as any other employee. In particular, there was no reason to distinguish between illnesses having their origin in pregnancy or childbirth and any other illness.

The importance of the European approach is that it regards treatment on grounds of pregnancy as sex-based discrimination, without any need to compare pregnant women with men. In the leading UK case of *Webb* v. *EMO Air Cargo (UK) Ltd* (1993)[10] the House of Lords looked at the difficult case of the dismissal of a woman who was taken on to provide temporary cover for another employee on maternity leave, who became pregnant, with the result that she would not be able to work at the relevant time. The House of Lords held that this was not discrimination under UK law, because a hypothetical man, unavailable at the relevant time because of a medical condition, would also have been dismissed. The precise reason for the unavailability was irrelevant. However, the House of Lords did rule that to dismiss a woman simply because of pregnancy, or to refuse to employ a woman of child-bearing age because she might become pregnant, would be sex discrimination. But where the reason is the consequences of the pregnancy, rather than pregnancy *per se*, then the comparison with a similarly incapacitated man must be made. Nevertheless, because of the uncertainty of the European law, the House of Lords decided to refer the case to the ECJ. The ECJ took a very different approach, and ruled that the dismissal of a pregnant woman recruited for an indefinite period was sex discrimination, and could not be justified on the grounds of a temporary inability to fulfil a fundamental term of her contract (ie to come to work). Under the Equal Treatment Directive it was unlawful to dismiss a woman on account of her pregnancy. Nor could pregnancy be equated in any way with sickness or unavailability for work on medical grounds. The House of Lords has since interpreted the SDA in accordance with the ruling of the ECJ in the case of a woman engaged for an indefinite period.

Regardless of the ECJ's decision in *Webb*, the comparison with a hypothetical sick man may have important implications for women. If it is sex discrimination to treat a pregnant employee less favourably than a man about to have a hernia operation, then many employers will need to examine their treatment of their pregnant employees. By and large, employers provide better sickness benefits than they do maternity benefits. Employees frequently qualify for sick pay after a short period of service, whereas more generous contractual maternity rights are only available after one or two years. Employees on sick leave may be entitled to keep company cars and other benefits, and pension entitlement and holiday entitlement may continue to accrue, rather than be frozen, as is common with maternity leave. There are signs that pregnant employees are beginning to see the advantages of comparing themselves with sick men. In *Reay* v. *Sunderland Health Authority* (1992)[11] a health visitor who returned to work after maternity leave was held to be entitled to time off in lieu for the bank holidays which had fallen during her absence, because men (and of course women) on sick leave were contractually entitled to time off in lieu. In *Gillespie* v. *Northern Health and Social Services Board* (1993)[12] a nurse received maternity pay, but this did not amount to full pay, nor was it recalculated to take account of a backdated pay rise. The Northern Ireland Court of Appeal has referred the case to the ECJ to see whether, under EC law, a woman on maternity

leave is entitled to receive the pay she would have received had she been
working normally.

Returning to work part time

The SDA 1975 has also been used by women who want to return to work
part time after having a baby. Although the statutory rights only guarantee the right to return to the woman's original job, it may amount to indirect sex discrimination to insist that the woman comes back full time.
The argument goes as follows. The employer imposes a requirement or
condition, that in order to return to work, the woman must come back
full time. The proportion of women who can comply with that requirement or condition is considerably smaller than the proportion of men
who can comply with it, because of women's greater childcare responsibilities. This requirement is to the woman's detriment. The crucial question is then whether the employer can justify the insistence that the job
be done full time. This will obviously vary from job to job. In the first
case on this point, *Home Office* v. *Holmes* (1984),[13] the Home Office
could not justify a requirement that a probation officer work full time, as
the work was done on a case-load basis. On the other hand, in *Gill* v.
Wirrall Health Authority (1991)[14] it was justifiable for a hospital to insist
that midwives in senior grades work full time, because of the level of
responsibility involved.

Maternity pay

The Government has introduced new maternity pay provisions, which
apply to all women expecting a baby on or after 16 October 1994.

All women who have been continuously employed in the same job for
26 weeks by the qualifying week are entitled to Statutory Maternity Pay.
They receive higher rate SMP (90 per cent of actual earnings) for the
first six weeks of their maternity leave, followed by up to 12 weeks at the
standard rate of SMP (which has been raised to the same level as SSP).

Employees without 26 weeks' continuous service receive the
Maternity Allowance, if they satisfy the contributions requirement. They
also have 66 weeks in which to satisfy the 26-week contributions
requirement, instead of 52 weeks.

Maternity leave and maternity pay can begin at any time after the
beginning of the 11th week before the expected week of childbirth. If a
woman is sick after this time, she will be able to claim SSP, rather than
SMP. However, if she is absent from work after the sixth week before
the baby is due, and her absence is due to a pregnancy-related cause,

then she will be deemed to be on maternity leave, and will receive SMP, not SSP.

This is a considerable improvement on previous provisions, and will be simpler to administer. However, it will be more expensive. The Government has decided that the cost should be borne by employers. This has been done by reducing the reimbursement rate from 104.5 per cent to 92 per cent. The Government has stated that this cost will be more than offset by reductions in employers' National Insurance contributions. Small employers (those paying less than £20,000 National Insurance contributions a year) will continue to be fully reimbursed.

Key points

- All pregnant employees are entitled to paid time off for antenatal care.
- All employees, regardless of length of service, will be entitled to 14 weeks' maternity leave.
- Employees with two years' continuous service retain entitlement to extended maternity leave.
- Notice provisions should be made clear to employees and strictly adhered to.
- In certain circumstances, either the employer or the employee can postpone return for up to four weeks.
- All rights can be improved by the contract.
- The right is to return to the old job.
- If there is a redundancy situation, the employer must offer the woman any available suitable alternative employment.
- Where it is necessary to suspend an employee for health and safety reasons, the employer should first look for alternative employment. Otherwise the woman must be suspended with pay.
- It is automatically unfair to dismiss a woman because of pregnancy, or because she takes maternity leave, regardless of length of service.
- It may be sex discrimination to treat a pregnant woman less favourably than a man on sick leave.
- It may be indirect sex discrimination to refuse to allow a woman to return to work part time.
- All women with 26 weeks' continuous employment by the qualifying week are entitled to six weeks' SMP at 90 per cent of their salary, followed by 12 weeks at standard rate SMP.

References

1 [1982] IRLR 180

2 [1984] IRLR 86
3 [1994] IRLR 270
4 [1988] IRLR 310
5 27 July 1993; Case No. 2688/91, unreported, see EOR-DCLD No. 18, p. 3
6 [1977] IRLR 327
7 [1993] IRLR 27
8 *Dekker* v. *Stichting Vormingcentrum voor Jonge Wolwassenen (VJV-Centrum) Plus* [1991] IRLR 27
9 *Hertz* v. *Aldi Marked K/S* [1991] IRLR 31
10 [1993] IRLR 27
11 Unreported, 30.12.92
12 Unreported, see IRLB 478, p. 15
13 [1984] IRLR 299
14 Unreported, 1991

Chapter 6
Equal pay

The average weekly earnings for women remain at around 70 per cent of average male earnings, although there is some evidence that the pay gap has begun to narrow. This is despite the fact that there has been equal pay legislation in the UK for almost 20 years. There are two main reasons for this: firstly, women tend to work in a sex-segregated job market; and secondly, skills traditionally associated with women are frequently undervalued. So women still tend to do 'women's jobs', and these are often underpaid in comparison with the jobs men tend to do. The success of equal pay legislation has to be measured against its effectiveness in tackling these problems, but the law can inevitably only have a limited effect in changing what are primarily structural problems in pay systems. The whole area of pay is inevitably problematic: why are certain jobs more highly rewarded than others? The best approach that employers can take in this area is to ensure that systems for setting pay are as objective as is possible and to check that the criteria used for setting pay do not have a hidden impact on women's pay rates.

Employers will find the EOC's new Code of Practice on equal pay useful in tackling the problem of pay inequality. The Code, laid before Parliament in October 1995, recommends that employers should adopt an equal pay policy. This involves carrying out an internal pay review, and the Code gives detailed guidance on how employers should conduct such a review. The EOC advises employers to examine various common elements of pay systems; it gives examples of potential discrimination and recommended action to deal with them. So employers should examine the operation of factors such as basic pay, bonus rates, performance-related pay, pay benefits and grading. The Code recommends that after undertaking the review and taking action to deal with any discrimination employers monitor the pay system regularly to ensure that discrimination does not creep back in. The Code of Practice is admissible as evidence in tribunal proceedings, but there is no legal obligation on employers to carry out a pay review or introduce an equal pay policy.

The Equal Pay Act 1970 (EqPA) did not come into force until 1975. The gap was intended to give employers time to implement its provisions, although some employers used the time to try to avoid the legislation by reclassifying women's jobs and altering job content! The Act

originally provided that women should receive equal pay with men in
two situations:

- where the woman was doing 'like work' with the man
- where the woman's job and the man's job had been rated as equivalent.

However, Article 119 of the Treaty of Rome requires that men and
women should receive equal pay for equal work, and in 1982 the
European Court of Justice (ECJ) ruled that the UK was in breach of its
Treaty obligations in this area. As a result the Act was amended by the
Equal Pay (Amendment) Regulations 1983 so that women could claim
equal pay for work of equal value.

The equality clause

The Act operates by inserting an 'equality clause' into the contract of
employment when a woman is employed on like work, work rated as
equivalent or work of equal value to that of a man. The equality clause
then modifies every term in the woman's contract which is less
favourable than the equivalent term in the man's contract, or adds a term
where the man's contract contains a term which is of benefit to him and
the woman has no corresponding term in her contract.

The equality clause applies to all contractual terms and conditions, not
just pay. So if the man has a company car, then the woman's contract is
modified so that she becomes entitled to a company car. It also applies
on a clause by clause basis, so that if a woman receives lower pay, then
her contract is modified, even though she might be entitled to more holiday, for example. In that situation, the man with whom she compared
herself could bring an equal pay claim to improve his holiday entitlement. The Act can be used in this way to improve pay packages overall.
In *Hayward* v. *Cammell Laird Shipbuilders (No.2)* (1988)[1] a woman
canteen cook claimed equal pay with male painters, thermal insulation
engineers, and joiners. Her work was found to be of equal value to theirs,
but the employer argued that overall she was receiving equal pay. Her
basic salary was lower, but she had better sick pay, paid meal breaks, and
extra holidays. The House of Lords rejected this approach, holding that
the legislation requires each individual term of the contract to be
improved, and if this leads to 'leapfrogging' claims, then so be it. This
approach was also followed by the ECJ in *Barber* v. *Guardian Royal
Exchange Assurance Group* (1990)[2] where it was held that giving Mr
Barber an enhanced severance payment did not justify the failure to pay
him an immediate pension: each element of the redundancy package had

to be equal.

Who can claim equal pay?

The EqPA 1970 applies to all those employed under a contract of service or of apprenticeship or a contract personally to execute any work or labour. This is similar to the terms of the Sex Discrimination Act 1975 (SDA) and covers the self-employed as well as employees, as long as the individual personally does the work in question. Crown employees are covered, except for those holding statutory office. Members of the armed forces are not covered, although this is almost certainly contrary to EC law. The Secretary of State for Defence is under an obligation not to make a distinction between the terms and conditions of men and women, unless that distinction is fairly attributable to differences between obligations undertaken. As in the SDA 1975, only employees working at an establishment in Great Britain are covered.

Exceptions

There are three exceptions, whose scope has been greatly reduced by EC law. The equality clause does not operate with regard to:

- terms affected by compliance with statutory restrictions relating to the employment of women. The SDA 1986 and the Employment Act 1989 have removed most of the protective legislation (see Chapter 3).
- terms giving women special treatment in relation to pregnancy or childbirth
- terms relating to death or retirement or any provision made in connection with death or retirement. However, following the *Barber* decision and its aftermath in the ECJ (see below), the equality clause does operate so as to apply an equal treatment rule to terms relating to membership of occupational pension schemes and the terms on which members are treated.

Time limits

There is no time limit for current employees in bringing a claim. However, there is uncertainty as to whether time limits apply in relation to former employees. In *British Railways Board* v. *Paul* (1989)[3] the Employment Appeal Tribunal (EAT) held that there was no time limit for former employees, unless the complaint had been referred by the Secretary of State, in which case a six-month time limit applies.

However, in *Etherson* v. *Strathclyde Regional Council* (1992)[4] the EAT held that the six-month time limit applied to all applications, and it is suggested that this is the better interpretation. In any event, there is a practical limit in that tribunals can only award arrears or damages in respect of the two years immediately before the proceedings were begun. So if an employee brings a claim a year after leaving employment, she can only be awarded the pay difference for one year. But it should be noted that there is no limit in EC law, and the ECJ ruled in *Marshall* v. *Southampton and South-West Hampshire Area Health Authority (No.2)* (1993)[5] that where the remedy is financial compensation, then this must be adequate, in the sense that the loss suffered by the individual must be made good in full. This obviously has enormous potential impact on equal pay claims, and can include a sum representing interest from the date of the discriminatory act.

However, in *Johnson* v. *Chief Adjudication Officer (No. 2)* (1995)[6] the ECJ ruled that national law can place a time limit in respect of the period over which a remedy may be claimed in arrears. The case involved a claim for a social security benefit, and it is not yet clear whether the two-year time limit on arrears under the EqPA is compatible with community law. The Occupational Pension Schemes (Equal Access to Membership) Regulations 1995 provide that claims for equal access to pension schemes are subject to the six-month time limit for bringing a claim where the applicant is an ex-employee, and the two-year limit on arrears of pay. There is also uncertainty over what time limits apply in relation to claims based on European law, and when those time limits begin to run (see Chapter 1).

The male comparator

Under the SDA 1975 a woman can claim that she has been less favourably treated than a hypothetical man. This is not possible under the EqPA 1970, where a woman has to find herself a real man to act as a comparator. If the employer employs no men, then the woman cannot bring her case, even if she feels that a man doing the job would be paid more.

However, a woman can claim equal pay with her male predecessor. In *McCarthys Ltd* v. *Smith* (1980)[7] Mrs Smith, a stockroom manager, claimed equal pay with the man who had previously done her job, but had left some months before she started. She was unable to claim under the EqPA 1970, but succeeded under Article 119. In *Dennehy* v. *Sealink Ltd* (1987)[8] a woman compared herself with a man who succeeded her in the job. However, in these circumstances, employers may be able to show that the difference in pay is justified as a 'genuine material differ-ence' on grounds other than sex.

The man must be 'in the same employment' as the woman. This means that the man must be employed by the same employer or any associated employer at the same establishment as the woman, or that the man is employed at a different establishment belonging to that employer or an associated employer where common terms and conditions of employment are observed, either generally or for employees of the relevant classes.

Associated employer

Employers are associated where one is a company which is controlled, directly or indirectly, by the other or where both are companies controlled, directly or indirectly, by a third party. However, in *Hasley* v. *Fair Employment Agency* (1989)[9] the Northern Ireland Court of Appeal held that this did not cover statutory bodies under the control of the government.

Common terms and conditions

In *Leverton* v. *Clwyd County Council* (1989)[10] a female nursery nurse claimed that her work was of equal value to that of male clerical workers employed by the local authority at different locations. The local authority argued that as there were significant differences in the terms and conditions of the two categories of employees, there were no common terms and conditions. The House of Lords disagreed, holding that the concept of common terms and conditions 'necessarily contemplates terms and conditions applicable to a wide range of employees whose individual terms will vary *inter se*'. Here, there were common terms and conditions because all the employees were covered by the same collective agreement. (Ms Leverton lost her case, however, as the difference in hours worked and holidays amounted to a 'genuine material difference' between her case and the men's.)

In *British Coal Corporation* v. *Smith; North Yorkshire County Council* v. *Ratcliffe* (1994)[11] the Court of Appeal held that 'common terms and conditions' means 'the same' terms and conditions, rather than 'broadly similar' or to the same overall effect. In the first case 1,286 women canteen workers and cleaners claimed equal pay with 150 male comparators (either surface miners or clerical workers). The Court of Appeal held that where the comparators worked at different establishments it was necessary to compare the terms of the male comparators with the terms of those men employed at the women's establishment, or the terms which would have applied if men had been working at the women's establishment. The selected male comparator should be representative of his group of employees. Here, no common terms existed because there were wide variations in the terms relating to incentive bonuses and concessionary coal.

In the second case, school catering assistants sought to compare themselves to road sweepers and refuse collectors. The jobs had been rated as equivalent under a job evaluation scheme in 1987, but following compulsory competitive tendering the Council set up direct service organisations (DSOs). The Court of Appeal ruled that despite the setting up of the DSOs, the men and women were in the same employment, because the men all enjoyed the same terms and conditions.

The number of comparators

At the moment, there is no restriction on the number of men that a woman can compare herself with. This is very useful, particularly in equal value claims, and many applicants use a 'scatter-gun' approach, comparing themselves with a number of men, all doing different jobs, in the hope that at least one will be held to be of equal value. However, there are signs that tribunals may begin to place limits on the number of comparators. In *British Coal Corporation* v. *Smith* (above), in which the applicants identified between 7 and 20 comparators, the EAT expressed concern that the citing of numerous comparators could amount to an oppressive tactic by applicants, who in many cases were supported by trade unions. This case was begun in 1985, and the EAT estimated that it was unlikely to be completed before 1998. The Government is considering amending the EqPA so that a woman can compare herself with only one man at a time. Applicants would still be able to name more than one comparator but would be required to put in separate claims, which could then be heard one after another.

Applicants can also use the discovery procedures, whereby tribunals order the employer to disclose details of pay rates and fringe benefits, as long as they can show a prima facie case of discrimination. In *Leverton* (above), the nursery nurse produced evidence, in the form of a recommendation from the Council and the union, that nursery nurses were underpaid in comparison with clerical officers. The industrial tribunal then ordered her employer to disclose details of the job descriptions and pay rates of male clerical officers, so that she could identify comparators.

Like work

The first situation in which women can claim equal pay is where a man is doing like work. Although there are relatively few claims under this head nowadays, like work does not mean identical work, and employees often bring claims based on like work and argue work of equal value as an alternative.

'Like work' is defined as work which is the same or of a *broadly similar nature*. Any differences which are not of practical importance between the things the woman does and the things the man does are to be ignored.

Broadly similar nature

Tribunals take a 'broad brush' approach and do not get bogged down in small details. In *Capper Pass Ltd* v. *Lawton* (1977)[12] a cook in a director's dining room and an assistant chef in the works canteen did work of a broadly similar nature.

The time at which the work is done is irrelevant – only what is done is relevant. So the basic pay for a day shift and night shift should be the same, although employers can pay a night shift premium to reflect the unsocial hours. This amounts to a genuine material difference, unrelated to sex. But if the night shift work has additional responsibilities, for example because of a lack of supervision, then the two jobs will not be 'like work'.

Differences

If the jobs are broadly similar in nature, then the tribunal will go on to examine the significance of any differences in what the woman and the man actually do. If there are differences, then are those differences of practical importance in relation to terms and conditions of employment? In other words, would a reasonable employer treat the differences as significant enough to justify placing the employees in different grades? Here, the focus is on what actually happens in practice: the fact that the job description or contract could require an employee to do different tasks is irrelevant. So in *Electrolux Ltd* v. *Hutchinson* (1976)[13] women and men on a production line were doing the same work, but the men were in a grade where they could be required to do night work, or be transferred to other departments. This was held to be irrelevant, unless they were in practice required to do night work to a significant extent.

Where there are significant differences between what the man does and what the woman does, tribunals must pay attention to how frequently the man is required to do different things. The occasional additional duty will be ignored.

Work rated as equivalent

Women can claim equal pay with men whose jobs have been rated as equivalent. In practice, this means that where an employer has undertaken a Job Evaluation Study (JES), and the woman's job has been placed in the same grade as the man's, then she is entitled to equal pay. JESs are also relevant to equal value claims, as an employer who can show that the woman's job and the man's have been rated differently has a prima facie defence, and may be able to have the case dismissed at a preliminary stage.

Job evaluation schemes are inherently problematic. Despite claims by management consultants that job evaluation is a science, it is inevitable that subjectivity creeps in. There is no objective standard for how much a particular job is worth; ultimately, pay rates are established by what the employer is prepared to pay, and what the employee is prepared to accept. Job evaluation has to be acceptable to both employers and employees, and a system which significantly alters existing perceptions of what a job is worth frequently does not work. Job evaluation is also relative: it is concerned with establishing differentials between different kinds of jobs, rather than setting concrete pay levels. That will be a matter for negotiation. The problem for equal pay is that the inevitable elements of subjectivity tend to reinforce the status quo, whereby the kind of work that is typically done by women tends to be undervalued *vis-à-vis* the type of work typically performed by men.

Nevertheless, job evaluation can improve the pay position of women, as it offers some mechanism for comparing the value of different jobs. Value here does not mean value to the employer, but what is required from the employee. It is the job that is valued, not the job holder. Section 1(5) of the EqPA 1970 refers to job evaluation 'in terms of the demand made on a worker under various headings (for instance effort, skill, decision)'. This clearly requires an analytical, factor-based scheme. There are various types of scheme, but it is widely recognised that the best schemes are those which reduce subjectivity as much as possible. The EAT, in an Appendix to its judgement in *Eaton Ltd* v. *Nuttall* (1977)[14] gave a guide to the most common forms of job evaluation:

- *Job Ranking*. This is commonly thought to be the simplest method. Each job is considered as a whole and is then given a ranking in relation to all other jobs. A ranking table is then drawn up and the ranked jobs grouped into grades. Pay levels can then be fixed for each grade.
- *Paired Comparisons*. This is also a simple method. Each job is compared as a whole with each other job in turn and points (0, 1 or 2) awarded according to whether its overall importance is judged to be less than, equal to or more than the other. Points awarded for each job are then totalled and a ranking order produced.
- *Job Classification*. This is similar to ranking except that it starts from the opposite end; the grading structure is established first and individual jobs fitted into it. A broad description of each grade is then drawn up and individual jobs considered typical of each grade are selected as

'benchmarks'. The other jobs are then compared with these benchmarks and the general description and placed in their appropriate grade.

- *Points Assessment.* This is the most common system in use. It is an analytical method, which, instead of comparing whole jobs, breaks down each job into a number of factors – for example, skills, responsibility, physical and mental requirements and working conditions. Each of these factors may be analysed further. Points are awarded for each factor according to a predetermined scale and the total points decide a job's place in the ranking order. Usually, the factors are weighted so that, for example, more or less weight may be given to hard physical conditions or to a high degree of skill.
- *Factor Comparison.* This is also an analytical method, employing the same principle as points assessment but using only a limited number of factors, such as skill, responsibility and working conditions. A number of 'key' jobs are selected because their wage rates are generally agreed to be 'fair'. The proportion of the total wage attributable to each factor is then decided and a scale produced showing the rate for each factor for each key job. The other jobs are then compared with this scale, factor by factor, so that a rate is finally obtained for each factor of each job. The total pay for each job is reached by adding together the rates for its individual factors.

Of these, job ranking, job pairing and job classification are generally agreed to be too subjective and not to satisfy the requirements of section 1(5) of the EqPA 1970.

If a woman's job and a man's job have been given the same value under a JES, then she is entitled to equal pay. It is not necessary for the scheme to be implemented. In *O'Brien* v. *Sim-Chem Ltd* (1980)[15] the employer carried out a JES, but did not implement it because of concern over the government's pay policy. The House of Lords held that Mrs O'Brien could claim equal pay with men placed in the same grade from the time when the employer told her of her new grade. However, in *Arnold* v. *Beecham Group Ltd* (1982)[16] a job evaluation was carried out with the involvement of the union, but when the results came out they proved unacceptable to the employees. The EAT held that a JES is not completed until it has been accepted by the parties as a valid study. Here, however, both union and employer had accepted that the study was substantially valid, and Miss Arnold was entitled to equal pay. But it is unclear what would happen if the study had been set up by management with no union involvement. Could the management, in effect, veto the scheme if they did not like the results and where those results would involve a pay rise for a substantial number of women? In such circumstances there would now be a very good case under the equal value provisions.

What exactly does 'rated as equivalent' mean? In *Springboard Sunderland Trust* v. *Robson* (1992)[17] Mrs Robson's job was rated at 410 points, her male comparator's job at 428 points. Salary Grade 4 ran from 410 points to 449, but Mrs Robson was placed in Grade 3, whereas the man was in Grade 4. The employer argued that the jobs had not been rated as equivalent, but the EAT disagreed: the JES involved the process whereby points were converted into grades, and so here the two jobs had been rated as equivalent.

JESs are often seen as a useful way for an employer to protect him or herself against an equal value claim. This is because, under the equal value provisions, the industrial tribunal must throw the case out at the preliminary stage (i.e. before appointing an independent expert) if the woman's job and the man's job have been given different values under a JES and there are no reasonable grounds for determining that the system used discriminated on the ground of sex. However, in order to provide the employer with this protection, the scheme has to be wide-ranging and, in particular, cut across traditional boundaries. Where the employer has one JES for blue-collar staff and another, separate system for white-collar staff, then this will do nothing to prevent an equal value claim being brought by a woman clerical officer comparing herself with a male warehouse employee.

It is also possible for employers to commission a JES after an equal value claim has been filed. In *Dibro Ltd* v. *Hoare* (1990)[18] the employer was allowed to introduce evidence of a JES carried out after equal value applications had been lodged with the tribunal, in order to show that there were no reasonable grounds for determining that the two jobs were of equal value.

It is also essential that the scheme used is not itself sex discriminatory. Section 2A(3) of the EqPA 1970 states that a system discriminates 'where a difference, or coincidence, between values set by that system on different demands under the same or different headings is not justifiable irrespective of the sex of the person on whom those demands are made'. What this rather convoluted wording means is that hidden, indirect discrimination within a JES will not prevent an equal value claim going ahead. The employer must be able to justify the choice of factors, and the weighting given to them.

To give a simple example, suppose a scheme gave physical strength a maximum score of 10 points, and manual dexterity a maximum of 5 points. This would be a difference between the values, and the employer would have to show that setting those different values was justifiable. Alternatively, a system might give physical conditions a maximum of 10 points, and qualifications a maximum of 10 points. This would be a coincidence between the values set, and again the employer would need to justify this. In the first example, the difference in values would lead to an overvaluation of a typically 'male' attribute, whereas in the second example, a female clerical officer with qualifications would find her job undervalued compared with a male warehouseman who worked in a less pleasant environment.

Employers should therefore be very careful about the kind of JES they use. The leading case is *Bromley* v. *H & J Quick Ltd* (1987)[19] where the employer commissioned a JES which ranked jobs by paired comparisons and then adjusted the ranking on a 'felt fair' basis. Jobs which had not been analysed were then slotted in and were only factor analysed if there was an appeal. The two women applicants had appealed, and so their jobs had been analysed, but the jobs of their male comparators had not. The Court of Appeal held that, in order to satisfy section 1(5) of the EqPA 1970 (and therefore protect against an equal value claim), the study must use analytical techniques to evaluate both the women's jobs and the men's. This scheme therefore did not satisfy that requirement. Even if the men's jobs had been factor analysed, it must still be doubtful as to whether the scheme would satisfy section 1(5), as the reclassifying of the jobs on a 'felt fair' basis introduces exactly those subjective views of what a particular job is worth which genuinely 'analytical' schemes should avoid. There is a tendency to reproduce conventional views as to what particular jobs are worth, and evidence suggests that this operates to the disadvantage of women.

Even if the JES rates the woman's job differently from the man's, she can still claim equal pay if the jobs would have been rated the same but for sex discrimination being built into the scheme. Section 1(5) limits this to direct sex discrimination – where the system sets different values for men and women, for example if men could score a maximum of 10 points for 'qualifications', but women could only score 5 points. However, EC law is relevant here, and women can challenge indirectly discriminatory JESs under Article 119 and the Equal Pay Directive 75/117. In *Rummler* v. *Dato-Druck GmbH* (1987)[20] the woman applicant argued that the use of muscular effort in a JES was discriminatory, as it failed to take account of physical exertion in relation to physical strength: in other words, women expended more effort than men in lifting the same weights. The ECJ rejected this, but did hold that where factors such as physical strength, which tend to favour men, are used, then the scheme should be designed, if possible, to take into account some factor which favours women, such as manual dexterity.

Equal value

Equal value claims have only been possible since the law was amended in 1984 and account for the majority of cases coming before the tribunals. There has been much criticism of the complexity and length of proceedings. In *British Coal Corporation* v. *Smith* (see p. 65) the EAT estimated that the case, begun in 1985, would not be completed until 1998, by which time it was statistically likely that many of the applicants would have died. Present procedures, according to the EAT, allow 'tactical manoeuvring by an employer, just as citation of such numerous comparators is capable of being an oppressive tactic of applicants'. The Government issued a Green Paper, 'Resolving employment rights disputes: options for reform', in 1995; this contains a number of proposals aimed at speeding up equal value claims.

An equal value claim is only relevant where the woman and her male comparator are not engaged on 'like work' or 'work rated as equivalent'. However, it is now clear that an employer cannot defeat an equal value claim by showing that there is another man engaged on like work or work rated as equivalent with the woman. In *Pickstone* v. *Freemans plc* (1987)[21] Mrs Pickstone, a warehouse operative, claimed equal value with a male 'checker warehouse operative'. But there were men employed alongside Mrs Pickstone as warehouse operatives, who were paid the same as she was. The House of Lords interpreted the Equal Value Regulations so as to give effect to Article 119 and the Equal Treatment Directive, and held that this meant that a woman was entitled to select her comparator. Only if she was actually engaged on like work with her chosen comparator should her claim be decided on the basis of like work. Otherwise employers would be able to destroy the purpose of equal value claims – to allow women to have their jobs compared with men doing different work – by employing a token man doing the same work as the woman.

Once a woman has filed an equal value claim, the tribunal holds a preliminary hearing. At this hearing, the tribunal must first offer to adjourn proceedings with a view to conciliation. If there is no adjournment, then the tribunal goes on to examine whether there is any point in referring the case to an independent expert, or whether the case should be dismissed at the preliminary stage. If the applicant has shown a prima facie case, then the tribunal can order discovery of relevant documents. This may enable the applicant to identify appropriate comparators and will allow her to establish their pay and other terms and conditions of employment. The tribunal can only throw the case out at this preliminary stage if there are 'no reasonable grounds for determining that the work is of equal value'. This is in addition to the general power of a tribunal to throw out cases which are 'frivolous or vexatious'. This power may be used where individuals want to pursue claims which are almost identical to earlier cases which have been thrown out: for example, where there are a number of claims filed by women doing the same jobs, and sample cases have already been dismissed. The Government announced in the Green Paper that it intends to abolish this power to throw cases out where there are 'no reasonable grounds'.

Apart from this power, there are three reasons why a tribunal might conclude that there are 'no reasonable grounds':

- If the case is so hopelessly weak that the tribunal is satisfied that it would be a waste of time and money to appoint an expert. The Government indicated when it introduced the equal value amendments that this power should be exercised sparingly.
- If the two jobs have been given different values under a JES, and there are no grounds to suspect that the JES was itself sex discriminatory (see above). This applies even where the JES was carried out after the woman filed her claim.
- If the employer can show that, even if the two jobs are of equal value, he has a valid defence, in that there is a genuine material factor, apart from sex, which justifies the pay differential. The employer can argue this defence at the preliminary hearing, and even if they are unsuccessful at this stage, there is nothing to prevent the same defence being argued again at the reconvened hearing. The Green Paper proposes that, in future, employers will be able to argue that there is a 'genuine material factor' defence only at the preliminary hearing (before any expert reports are commissioned) and that the defence can be considered at the reconvened hearing only in exceptional circumstances.

If the tribunal does not dismiss the case at the preliminary stage, then they must appoint an independent expert, selected from a panel chosen by ACAS. The expert has considerable discretion in how they go about comparing the two jobs, and there is evidence of considerable variation in how different experts go about the task. The Industrial Tribunals (Rules of Procedure) Regulations 1985 state that the expert must 'take account of all such information supplied and all such representations made to him as have a bearing on the question', that before drawing up his report he should send to the parties a summary of the information and representations, and invite their comments, and that he should take no account of the difference of sex and at all times act fairly. It is also clear that the expert must carry out an analytical comparison based on the demands made on the applicant and her comparators. But the expert only compares the jobs in question: he does not carry out a general job evaluation scheme.

The expert is supposed to produce his report within 42 days, but in practice they generally take considerably longer. New Rules of Procedure came into force on 16 December 1993 and the expert is now required to give written notice (within 14 days of being required to prepare the report) of the date by which he or she expects to send the report to the tribunal. If the expert considers at any time that there will be a material delay in delivering the report they must notify the tribunal accordingly, together with the reasons for the delay. The tribunal can require the expert at any time to submit a progress report on any delays, and if the tribunal considers that there will be an unjustifiable delay, they can require a report from a new expert. Once the report is done, the expert must send it to the tribunal. The report must contain a summary of the information received, a brief account of the representations from the parties, and any conclusion reached together with reasons. The tribunal then holds a resumed hearing.

At the resumed hearing, the first issue is whether to admit the expert's report as evidence. It is important to realise that a report can be admitted as evidence, but the tribunal can then go on to reach a different conclusion from that contained in the report. If the tribunal rejects the expert's report, then it must commission another report; it cannot decide the case without admitting an expert's report as evidence. The tribunal cannot reject the report simply because it disagrees with the conclusion: the report can only be rejected because the expert has failed to comply with the correct procedure or because the conclusion reached is perverse, in the sense that no reasonable expert could have reached it, or because the report is unsatisfactory for some other material reason.

It is now clear that, although the expert's report is obviously important evidence, it is not conclusive. In *Tennants Textile Colours Ltd* v. *Todd* (1989)[22] the Northern Ireland Court of Appeal ruled that the burden of proof remains on the applicant to show, on a balance of probabilities, that her work is of equal value with her comparators. Just because the expert's report goes against her, her burden is no heavier. Nor if the report is in her favour does the burden of proof shift towards the employer. The importance of this in practice is that both employer and applicant can commission their own 'expert's report', and these experts' reports can be of equal weight to that of the independent expert.

Either party can cross-examine the independent expert, and each party can call one expert witness of their own. It is important to challenge any findings of fact in the independent expert's report before it is admitted as evidence, as afterwards the parties cannot challenge any fact on which a conclusion is based, unless that evidence relates to the 'genuine material factor' defence, or the expert failed to reach a conclusion because the parties did not provide the relevant information. Once the report is admitted as evidence, it is for the tribunal to decide whether the two jobs are of equal value. But if the report is not admitted as evidence, the whole process starts all over again and another expert report must be commissioned. All this is to change. The Government has announced its intention of removing the requirement for an independent expert to be appointed, and instead intends to give the tribunal a discretion as to whether or not to require an expert report.

The employer's defence

Assuming that the tribunal holds that the two jobs are of equal value, the employer then has a chance to show that the pay differential is nevertheless justified:

- In relation to 'like work' and 'work rated as equivalent' claims, the employer has to show that the variation in pay is genuinely due to a 'material difference between the woman's case and the man's' which is not the difference of sex.
- For equal value claims, the employer must show that the difference is genuinely due to a 'material factor' (other than the difference of sex) which may or may not amount to a 'material difference'.

The difference in wording was originally designed to allow defences such as market forces apply to equal value claims, but following the decision of the House of Lords in *Rainey* v. *Greater Glasgow Health Board* (1987)[23] it now seems that there is little real difference between the defences. Material factors, such as market forces, can also amount to material differences between the woman's case and the man's.

In *Rainey* female artificial limb fitters, employed by the NHS, claimed equal pay with male limb fitters who had previously been employed in the private sector. In order to attract these men to transfer to the NHS, they had been offered higher rates of pay. All subsequent new employees were paid at the lower rate of pay. The House of Lords held that this was a material difference: 'where there is no question of intentional sex discrimination whether direct or indirect . . . a difference which is connected with economic factors affecting the efficient carrying on of the employer's business or other activity may well be relevant'.

Rainey also makes it clear that European law is relevant. In *Bilka-Kaufhaus GmbH* v. *Weber von Hartz* (1986)[24] the ECJ held that it was unlawful to exclude part-time workers (predominantly female) from an occupational pension scheme unless the employer could show that the exclusion was based on 'objectively justified factors unrelated to any discrimination on the ground of sex'. This requires an employer to show that the exclusion was done to meet a 'real need on the part of the undertaking, [was] appropriate with a view to achieving the objective . . . and . . . was necessary to that end'. The House of Lords held that this test was also relevant under section 1(3) of the EqPA 1970. In other words, employers must show some objective justification for differences in pay between workers whose work is of equal value. However, tribunals have not applied this principle in a uniform manner, and the law is still developing. Several important cases have been referred to the ECJ, and it is to be hoped that some useful guidance will be given on exactly how and when the defence is established.

Examples of genuine material differences/material factors

Geographic weighting
Where employees can bring cross-establishment comparisons, then an employer may be able to rely on differences in cost of living in different parts of the country to explain the pay differential, assuming that this is not due to any direct or indirect sex discrimination.

Market forces
Rainey established that market forces can justify pay differentials. In that case, the House of Lords indicated that as well as showing a good reason for paying men more, it may also be necessary to show grounds why the women should be paid less – i.e. why their pay should not be brought up to the men's rate. In *Rainey* the House of Lords accepted that there were administrative reasons for keeping the women on the usual NHS scale rates. The difficulty with market forces as a defence is that it tends to reproduce existing accepted pay rates for particular kinds of work, which is exactly what equal value law is intended to attack. For example, it should not be objectively justifiable for an employer to show that he paid a lower rate for a job done predominantly by women, because women were prepared to work for lower wages.

The other problem with the market forces defence arises in cases where market forces explain some, but not all, of the pay differential. In *Enderby* v. *Frenchay Health Authority and Secretary of State for Health* (1992)[25] speech therapists in the NHS claimed equal pay with pharmacists, amongst others. The speech therapists were predominantly female, and the pharmacists predominantly male. The NHS argued that this was because of market forces: pharmacists could work in the private sector and needed to be paid more in order to attract them. However, it was established that only some 10 per cent of the pay differential could be explained by shortages of pharmacists. The Court of Appeal referred the case to the ECJ, asking whether this justified all, part, or none of the pay differential. The ECJ has ruled that if only part of the pay difference is accounted for by the need to attract suitably qualified candidates to the job, then only that part of the difference is justified. But it is up to the national court to quantify how much of the difference is attributable to market forces.

However, market forces cannot justify a pay differential when the market forces themselves are tainted with sex discrimination. In *North Yorkshire County Council* v. *Ratcliffe* (1995)[26] female catering assistants, whose work had been rated equivalent to that of male roadsweepers and refuse collectors, had their pay reduced when the Council set up a Direct Service Organisation for catering in order to compete with private companies submitting tenders for the school meals service. The House of Lords ruled that although this was a genuine material factor, it was tainted with sex discrimination. The labour market here was sex-segregated, and the wages of the women were reduced in order to allow the Council to compete with private employers who also employed women predominantly. The wages were low because the employees were women, who could not have found other suitable jobs and were obliged to take the wages offered if they wanted to continue working in these jobs, which fitted in with child care and other family responsibilities.

Different pay structures and collective bargaining arrangements
Equal value claims clearly have the potential to cut through traditional pay structures, such as having one pay scale for blue-collar workers and another for white-collar workers. However, employers also seek to rely on the existence of separate pay scales, or different collective bargaining arrangements, to justify pay differentials. Does this amount to a genuine material factor? Obviously, if the grading system or collective bargaining process is itself tainted with sex discrimination, then it will not be a defence. In *Longman* v. *Lloyds Bank plc* (1989)[27] female clerical and secretarial staff claimed equal pay with male messengers. There were separate collective bargaining arrangements covering the two groups of workers, but the tribunal found that the collective bargaining process had been influenced in the past by notions of the 'family wage', and therefore this was not a material factor unconnected with sex.

In *Reed Packaging Ltd* v. *Boozer and Everhurst* (1988)[28] the EAT held that the existence of two separate pay scales for clerks and manual workers, negotiated with different unions, did amount to a genuine material difference, as neither pay scale was discriminatory itself and they were 'administratively justified'. Again, this appears to be exactly the sort of pay structure that equal value law is designed to challenge.

A better approach was taken in *Barber* v. *NCR (Manufacturing) Ltd* (1993)[29] where the EAT held that it is not enough for an employer to show that the cause of the variation was free from sex discrimination. So here different collective bargaining arrangements merely explained the historical process whereby women were paid less than men, but did not justify or even support that pay differential. The employer needs to show a material factor which justifies the pay differential.

This approach has now received support from the decision of the ECJ in the *Enderby* case (see above). The speech therapists also claimed that their work was of equal value to that of clinical psychologists in the NHS, who were predominantly male. The defence here was that the pay differential could be explained by different collective bargaining arrangements, which were not themselves tainted by sex discrimination. The Court of Appeal asked the ECJ the following questions:

1. Does the principle of equal pay in Article 119 require the employer to

objectively justify the difference in pay between job A and job B, where job A is done predominantly by women, and job B is done predominantly by men?
2. If the employer is required to justify the difference, can they rely on non-discriminatory collective agreements to justify the difference in pay?

The ECJ has ruled that employers must show objective justification, and that collective bargaining arrangements do not justify pay differences, even if the bargaining process is untainted either by direct or indirect discrimination. In future, employers will have to justify different pay scales, rather than simply explain how they arose.

The *Enderby* case develops the approach taken by the ECJ in two important cases on collective bargaining. In *Kowalska* v. *Freie und Hansestadt Hamburg* (1990)[30] the ECJ ruled that a collective agreement which excluded part-time workers from severance payments was indirectly discriminatory and would be unlawful under Article 119 unless the employers could justify the exclusion of part-timers by objective factors unrelated to sex. Any collective agreement that does not provide pro-rata benefits for part-timers will be indirectly discriminatory and cannot be relied upon as a justification.

In *Nimz* v. *Freie und Hansestadt Hamburg* (1991)[31] a provision in a collective agreement meant that full-timers were moved to a higher pay scale after six years, whereas part-timers had to work longer. The ECJ held that this was indirect discrimination and that the employer had to justify it by showing a 'relationship between the nature of the duties performed and the experience afforded by the performance of those duties after a certain number of working hours having been worked'. Again, the fact that the rule was set out in a collective agreement was not, in itself, a justification.

Grading differences and pay systems

Employers frequently operate pay systems which award increments on the basis of a variety of factors: length of service, training and qualifications, productivity, merit, performance-related pay, and so on. These factors may operate in such a way that women overall are paid less than men. In the *Danfoss* case (1989)[32] the ECJ ruled that, where the average pay of women workers is lower than the average pay of male workers, and the pay system is not 'transparent' (i.e. it is not clear exactly why such a differential exists), then the burden of proof falls on the employer to show that the pay system is not sex discriminatory by justifying the use of the various criteria used to establish pay. In *Danfoss*, the employer relied on flexibility (meaning variation in hours and locations): this was indirectly discriminatory, because of women's family responsibilities, and therefore had to be objectively justified, as did the use of vocational training. However, the ECJ was prepared to accept that length-of-service increments did not have to be justified by evidence, as there was a presumption that experience clearly enabled a worker to perform their job better. However, in *Nimz*, the ECJ changed their mind, and held that seniority does not, in itself, justify pay differentials; there must be some relationship between experience and performance.

So employers should check their pay systems to ensure that the criteria used to decide an employee's position on a pay scale are clear and can be objectively justified, in the sense that they meet some real business need. Placing an employee on a higher pay level just because they have a Masters degree may well be unjustifiable, whereas doing so for attending a job-related training course may be fine. Seniority awards may be justified as a means of achieving staff loyalty and reducing turnover and training costs, but it may be harder to justify them in terms of improved performance: in many jobs employees will achieve maximum performance in a relatively short period of time.

Performance-related pay may be the next big issue in equal pay. Once flavour of the month, there is now evidence that performance-related pay can, in fact, have a demoralising effect on staff performance. From an equal pay perspective, it is the large element of subjectivity in many systems, and the lack of uniformity in the way in which they operate within different divisions of the same organisation, that have led people to question whether they have a disproportionate impact on women's pay levels. Employers should be careful to ensure that performance-related pay is operated in as objective a way as possible and that any disparities in the internal operation of such systems are ironed out. Check whether women's average pay levels are lower than men's, then find out why. If the employer cannot show some good business-related reason which is being met by the system, then change it.

In *Specialarbejderforbundet i Danmark* v. *Dansk Industri acting for Royal Copenhagen* (1995)[33] the ECJ held that the principle of equal pay in Article 119 and the Equal Pay Directive apply to piece work systems, so that the pay of two groups of workers, one predominantly female and one predominantly male, had to be calculated according to the same 'unit of measurement'. This does not mean that the two groups need to receive the same pay, but the difference must be due to different individual output. Again, as in the *Danfoss* case, the ECJ held that where the pay system is lacking in transparency, the burden of proof shifts to the employer to show the differences in pay are due to objectively justified factors unconnected with sex.

Red circling
Employers sometimes choose to personally protect an individual's salary, even though they are doing a job with a lower rate of pay. This

may happen in a redundancy situation, where an employee is 'bumped' into a lower grade, or an employee may transfer to a lower paid job as a result of ill health. The true rate for the job is recognised to be the lower rate, but the employee's pay is 'red-circled' – personally protected. This may last for as long as the employee continues to work for the employer, or it may be temporary, with the higher pay rate gradually disappearing with the effect of inflation and pay rises.

The difficulty arises when a woman, often doing 'like work', claims equal pay with a man within the red circle. It is clear that a genuine red-circle case can amount to a material difference; however, it is essential that the red circling itself is not sex discriminatory. In *Snoxell and Davies* v. *Vauxhall Motors Ltd* (1978)[34] women quality controllers were in a lower grade, and paid less, than male quality controllers, prior to the EqPA 1970 coming into force. Following the Act, a unisex grade was established at the lower rate, but all the men who had previously been in the higher grade had their pay 'red-circled'. This was not a defence, because it was based on sex discrimination: but for their sex, the women would have been in the higher grade and had their pay red-circled too.

A difficult issue is how long the red circle should last. In *Charles Early and Marriot (Witney) Ltd* v. *Smith and Ball* (1977)[35] a man's job was downgraded, but his higher level of pay was personally protected. The EAT held that there was no sex discrimination to the red circle and that it would be a good defence, even if it were to continue indefinitely. Although in principle this is a logical decision, the approach of the tribunals is that red circling is justified in the interests of good industrial relations, but that in the further interest of those relations it is better that red circling is phased out: people tend to forget the original reason for Mr X being paid more than Ms Y. In *Outlook Supplies Ltd* v. *Parry* (1978)[36] a red circle which continued for two and a half years was thrown out as a defence by an industrial tribunal: the case was sent back by the EAT for the tribunal to consider whether the employer had, in fact, acted in accordance with good industrial relations. It will be much easier to defend a temporary red circle.

Employers should also ensure that no new employees are allowed into the red circle. In *United Biscuits Ltd* v. *Young* (1978)[37] men on the night shift were paid a higher basic wage than women on the day shift, allegedly because of a 'responsibility allowance', although the extra responsibility had since disappeared. However, two men had been taken on since the responsibility had disappeared, and this prevented the defence from succeeding.

Financial problems
Where this genuine material factor no longer exists, it cannot justify continuing pay differences. In *Beneveniste* v. *Southampton University*

(1989)[38] a woman was recruited at a time of severe financial cutbacks in universities and, as a result, was appointed six points below the appropriate wage for her age on the pay scale. By the time she brought her case, the financial constraints had eased, and it was held that the material difference no longer applied.

Pensions

Pension schemes are a complex and uncertain area in terms of equal pay. It is important to distinguish between the State pension scheme (including SERPS), where discrimination is allowed under EC law, as this is based on different pensionable ages for men and women, and occupational pension schemes. The latter were originally excluded from the operation of the EqPA 1970, in the same way that discriminatory retirement ages were excluded from the SDA 1975 (see Chapter 3).

The Social Security Act 1975 makes it unlawful to discriminate on the ground of sex in terms of access to pension schemes, so that there can be no distinction between men and women as to the age at which they can join schemes, or the length of service required. The Social Security Act 1975 covered only *direct* discrimination with regards to access to pension schemes, but the ECJ ruled in *Bilka-Kaufhaus*[39] that Article 119 covered the right to join a pension scheme, and that it could amount to indirect discrimination to refuse to allow part-timers to join a pension scheme where more women than men were affected, and the employer could not objectively justify refusing to let part-timers join the scheme. In two important decisions in 1994, *Vroege*[40] and *Fisscher*[41], the ECJ confirmed that to refuse part-timers access to the pension scheme could amount to indirect sex discrimination, and went on to hold that unlike the right to equal benefits under the pension scheme (see discussion of *Barber* below) there was no time limit on bringing a backdated claim. These rulings opened up the possibility of part-timers who had been refused access to the pension scheme bringing claims seeking backdated membership from April 1976. An estimated 75,000 claims have since been filed in the UK.

There are two important limitations on such claims. Firstly, if the scheme is contributory, then the ECJ suggested that part-timers would have to pay any employee contributions due. This would obviously be problematic for many part-timers. Secondly, the ECJ held that national time limits for bringing claims would apply. Existing employees will therefore be able to bring claims, but former employees will probably be subject to the six-month time limit under the Equal Pay Act 1970. The crucial question is, when does the time limit begin to run? It can be argued that the six-month time limit should run only from 28 September

1994, when the ECJ gave their decisions in *Vroege* and *Fisscher*: until that date it would be unreasonable to expect a part-timer to know that she had any rights under Article 119. But in *Biggs* v. *Somerset County Council* (1995)[42] the EAT held that where a claim was brought on the basis of Article 119, the time limit should run from the date of the discriminatory act – here, when the employee left her job. This uncertainty in the current law is highly unsatisfactorily.

However, as a result of these rulings, the Government introduced the Occupational Pension Schemes (Equal Access to Membership) Regulations 1995. These Regulations came into force on 31 May 1995, and provide that all forms of discrimination, both direct and indirect, are outlawed with respect to access to pension schemes. So where there is a rule that excludes individuals who work fewer than a certain number of hours a week, and this disproportionately affects women, this is unlawful unless it can be justified on objective grounds. The new Regulations apply the six-month time limit for ex-employees, but also provide that any award made by a Tribunal can be backdated for only two years. Where an employer has continued to exclude part-timers from the pension scheme after 31 May 1995, and this has been found to be unlawful, then the employer will be required to pay both the employer's and the employee's contributions. It is arguable that the two-year limit on back pay contravenes European law, following the *Marshall* judgement. (See Chapter 2.)

The Social Security Act 1989 was intended to further equalise occupational pension schemes by January 1993, but the provisions of the Act were overtaken by events: in the landmark decision of *Barber* v. *Guardian Royal Exchange Assurance Group* (1990)[43] the ECJ ruled that benefits under contracted-out occupational pension schemes were 'pay' under Article 119 and therefore must be equal for men and women. This judgement has so far raised as many questions as it answers.

Mr Barber was a member of a non-contributory pension scheme, with a pensionable age of 62 for men and 57 for women. Employees were entitled to an immediate pension 'on being retired' within 10 years of pensionable age. Mr Barber was made redundant aged 52: the redundancy scheme stated that men over 55 and women over 50 were 'retired', so that they were entitled to an immediate pension. Mr Barber received an enhanced redundancy payment, but claimed that this was sex discrimination: but for his sex, he would have received an immediate pension.

The ECJ made the following rulings:

- All redundancy payments are 'pay' under Article 119, whether statutory, contractual, or ex gratia.
- Contracted-out occupational pension benefits are 'pay' under Article 119. It is irrelevant that pension schemes are run by trustees.

- It is contrary to Article 119 to pay a lesser pension to a man than to a woman, even though this is based on different pensionable ages set under the state scheme.
- Each and every element of the redundancy package must be equal. It is not open to the employer to reduce certain elements (here the right to an immediate pension) and enhance others.
- Article 119 has direct effect and can be relied on in national courts by all employees, whether employed by 'the State' or private employers.

The ECJ recognised that the financial implications of the *Barber* decision would be enormous, and therefore took the unusual step of ruling that its decision was not to have retrospective effect. It was stated that 'the direct effect of Article 119 may not be relied on in order to claim entitlement to a pension with effect from a date prior to that of this judgement', with the exception of workers who had instituted legal proceedings already. The date of the *Barber* judgement was 17 May 1990.

However, there was considerable disagreement as to what this provision meant. Did it mean that any pension which became payable after 17 May 1990 must be equal for men and women, or did it mean that equality only applied to that part of the pension earned after 17 May 1990? If the former, then the immediate costs for pension schemes would be enormous; if the latter, then it would be 40 years from the date of the judgement before real equality existed in pension schemes.

Following *Barber*, a number of cases concerning various aspects of pension schemes were referred to the ECJ. The most important of these was the *Coloroll* case (1993)[44] which arose following the winding up of the Coloroll group's pension schemes. The trustees of the scheme sought guidance from the High Court, who referred a number of questions to the ECJ.

- The *Coloroll* case, together with nine others before the ECJ, now provides clearer guidance on what is, and what is not, permissible in occupational pension schemes. It is now clear that all benefits payable under occupational pension schemes need to be equalised only with respect to benefits payable in respect of service *after* 17 May 1990. The Maastricht Treaty of 1993 contained Protocol 2, to the same effect. The reasoning was that before this date it was reasonable for those running pension schemes to make calculations about the financial basis for such schemes based on different pension schemes for men and women.
- The Court has also held that the use of sex-based actuarial tables in a final salary scheme is lawful under Article 119. So employee contributions, deducted from salary, must be the same for men and women, but employers' contributions, which are designed to ensure that there is

enough money in the pension fund to meet future liabilities, do not constitute pay, and therefore do not fall within Article 119. So transfer payments, commutation payments and lump sums payable do not need to be the same for men and women. It is still unclear whether this principle applies to money purchase or defined contribution schemes.

- Survivors' benefits are pay under Article 119 in relation to periods of service post-*Barber*.
- Bridging pensions, whereby the employer reduces a woman's pension between 60 and 65 because of the State pension, are not contrary to Article 119, because this is a measure designed to eliminate inequality.[45]
- Article 119 does not apply to Additional Voluntary Contributions (AVCs).[46]
- Benefits after 17 May 1990 can be reduced to achieve equality. There is no need for schemes to level benefits upwards. But between 17 May 1990 and the date the scheme is equalised, any equalisation must be upwards. So transitionary arrangements designed to limit the effects of levelling down are unlawful. Equalisation must be immediate and full.[47]

The Pensions Act 1995 has introduced a common pension age for men and women, to be phased in between 2010 and 2020. It also requires equal treatment for men and women in pension schemes, as required by European Community law.

Key points

- Check pay systems for objectivity.
- Examine pay systems for any hidden impact on women's pay levels.
- Equality clauses raise each and every contract term, not just pay.
- Where an employer has more than one establishment, check the possibility of cross-establishment claims.
- Job Evaluation Systems will only protect against equal value claims if they are free of both direct and indirect sex discrimination, and cover all categories of employee.
- It is possible to introduce a JES even after an equal pay claim has been filed.
- In an equal value claim, employers can argue the 'material factor' defence at the preliminary hearing, before an expert's report is commissioned.
- Employers should challenge any findings of fact in an independent expert's report before the tribunal admits the report as evidence.
- 'Genuine material factors' need to objectively justify pay differentials.

Employers cannot simply rely upon the existence of different collective bargaining arrangements or pay systems, market forces or red circles.

- Check that any performance-related pay does not discriminate against women, directly or indirectly.
- Pension schemes should provide equal benefits for men and women, at least in respect of service after 17 May 1990.

References

 1 [1988] AC 894
 2 [1990] IRLR 240
 3 [1989] IRLR 20
 4 [1992] IRLR 392
 5 [1993] IRLR 445
 6 [1995] IRLR 157
 7 [1980] IRLR 210
 8 [1987] IRLR 120
 9 [1989] IRLR 106
10 [1989] IRLR 28
11 [1994] IRLR 343
12 [1977] QB 852
13 [1976] IRLR 410
14 [1977] IRLR 71
15 [1980] IRLR 373
16 [1982] IRLR 307
17 [1992] IRLR 261
18 [1990] IRLR 129
19 [1987] IRLR 456
20 [1987] IRLR 32
21 [1987] IRLR 357
22 [1989] IRLR 3
23 [1987] IRLR 26
24 [1986] IRLR 317
25 [1992] IRLR 15
26 [1995] IRLR 439
27 1989 IDS Brief 15
28 [1988] IRLR 332
29 [1993] IRLR 95
30 [1990] IRLR 447
31 [1991] IRLR 222
32 *Handels- og Kontorfunktionaerernes Forbund i Danmark* v. *Dansk Arbejdsgiverforening (Danfoss case)* [1989] IRLR 532

33 31 May 1995, Case C 400/93
34 [1978] 1 QB 11
35 [1977] IRLR 123
36 [1978] IRLR 12
37 [1978] IRLR 15
38 [1989] IRLR 122
39 *Bilka-Kaufhaus GmbH* v. *Weber von Hartz* [1986] IRLR 317
40 *Vroege* v. *NCIV Instituut voor Volkshuisvesting BV and another*
    [1994] IRLR 616
41 *Fisscher* v. *Voorhuis Hengelo BV and another* [1994] IRLR 662
42 [1995] IRLR 452; see Chapter 1
43 [1990] IRLR 240
44 *Coloroll Pension Trustees Ltd* v. *Russell, Mangham and others*
    [1991] IRLIB 431; ECJ [1994] IRLR 586
45 *Roberts* v. *Birds Eye Walls Ltd* [1994] IRLR 29
46 *Coloroll* [1994] IRLR 586
47 *Smith* v. *Advel Systems Ltd* [1994] IRLR 602

Chapter 7
Race discrimination

Ethnic minorities form 4.9 per cent of the working population in the UK. However, there is considerable evidence of widespread racial discrimination in employment. Not only is the level of unemployment substantially higher for ethnic minorities (13 per cent compared with 7 per cent), but ethnic minorities are concentrated in low-level jobs at low rates of pay. As with sex discrimination, employers who wish to ensure that they get the best employee for the job – and to develop the full potential of existing employees – need to develop equal opportunity programmes that specifically address the issue of race.

The law on racial discrimination is contained in the Race Relations Act 1976 (RRA). The Act was modelled on and closely followed the Sex Discrimination Act 1975 (SDA). The case law on sex discrimination is good authority for interpreting the parallel provisions on race discrimination, and vice versa. The Commission for Racial Equality (CRE) has similar powers and functions to the Equal Opportunities Commission (EOC) and has issued a useful Code of Practice for the Elimination of Racial Discrimination and the Promotion of Equality of Opportunity in Employment.

The EC has no specific measures on race discrimination, although Article 48 of the Treaty of Rome guarantees the free movement of workers between the Member States. There has recently been much concern over the issue of racial discrimination within the EC, and the Commission and Parliament have both indicated that serious consideration should be given to a Directive to provide a Community framework of legislation on racial discrimination.

What is race discrimination?

Direct discrimination

The RRA 1976, like the SDA 1975, outlaws both direct and indirect discrimination. Direct discrimination occurs when a person treats someone, on racial grounds, less favourably than they treat or would treat another person.

The RRA 1976 specifically states that segregation on racial grounds is

less favourable treatment. So this would cover an employer who provides separate, but equal, toilet facilities, for example. However, it
appears that, to be unlawful, the segregation must be deliberate. In
Furniture, Timber and Allied Trades Union v. *Modgill: Pel Ltd* v.
Modgill (1980)[1] only Asians were employed in the paint shop, which
involved dirty and unpleasant work. The Asian workers alleged, amongst
other things, that the employer was discriminating by way of segregation. The Employment Appeal Tribunal (EAT) held that, if this was a
deliberate company policy, then it would be discrimination. But here the
evidence was that the workers themselves operated a system whereby, if
one was leaving, he would tell his (Asian) friends or relatives, who
would then apply for the job. The employer had not advertised a job in
the paint shop for more than two years. There was no deliberate segregation. However, an employer committed to genuine equal opportunities
should ensure that word-of-mouth recruitment is not used, as it tends to
reproduce the same ethnic (and indeed sex) group.

It is irrelevant whether the employer was motivated by racial prejudice
or not. If the treatment was based on racial grounds, that is enough. In *R.*
v. *Commission for Racial Equality ex parte Westminster City Council*
(1985)[2] the Council appointed a black refuse collector, but then with-
drew his appointment because there was concern that the other (white)
refuse collectors would take industrial action. This was racial discrimination, because the decision was taken on racial grounds, even though the
motive was to avoid industrial action.

As with sex discrimination, it is clear that many employers do discriminate directly on the ground of race. However, such 'direct' discrimination is usually hidden; it is very unusual for an employer to tell an
applicant that they have been refused a job because of their race. The difficulty for the individual who suspects that this is the reason for their
treatment is that they have the burden of proof in the tribunal. Although
tribunals have shown themselves to be sensitive to this issue and will
look to the employer for an explanation if there is some evidence of less
favourable treatment, it is nevertheless difficult to prove direct racial discrimination in the absence of some incriminating remark or comment.

What are 'racial grounds'?
'Racial grounds' means 'on the grounds of colour, race, nationality, ethnic or national origin'. Most of the case law has centred on the meaning
of the words 'ethnic origin'. The leading case is *Mandla* v. *Dowell Lee*
(1983).[3] A headmaster of a private school refused to admit a Sikh boy
because he insisted on wearing a turban, rather than the school cap. The
Court of Appeal ruled that this was religious discrimination and that
'ethnic' meant the same as 'racial'. The case was unanimously overruled
by the House of Lords, who held that Sikhs were indeed an ethnic group.

In order for a group to be seen as an ethnic group there are two essential characteristics:

(1) a long shared history, of which the group is conscious as distinguishing it from other groups, and the memory of which it keeps alive;
(2) a cultural tradition of its own, including family and social customs and manners – often, but not necessarily associated with religious observance.

In addition, the following characteristics are relevant:

(3) either a common geographical origin or descent from a small number of common ancestors;
(4) a common language, not necessarily peculiar to that group;
(5) a common literature, peculiar to that group;
(6) a common religion different from that of neighbouring groups or from the general community surrounding it;
(7) being a minority or being an oppressed or a dominant group within a larger community, for example a conquered people . . . and their conquerors might both be ethnic groups . . .

The Court of Appeal has since held that gypsies are an ethnic group, as a minority with a long shared history and a common geographical origin.[4] However, Rastafarians are not: the Court of Appeal held that there was nothing to set them apart from the rest of the Jamaican or Afro-Caribbean community. Nor was their shared history long enough, going back only 60 years.[5] There are also industrial tribunal decisions holding that Muslims are not an ethnic group. However, this does not mean that employers can advertise jobs as available only to non-Muslims or non-Rastafarians, as this raises issues of indirect racial discrimination.

Discrimination on grounds of another's race
It has also been held to be racial discrimination where someone is discriminated against because of someone else's colour or race. In *Zarczynska* v. *Levy* (1978)[6] a woman was sacked because she served a black customer, when the employer had expressly told her not to. In a rather broad interpretation of the RRA 1976, the EAT held that this was discrimination on racial grounds.

Indirect discrimination

Indirect discrimination is defined by section 1(1)(b) as occurring when a person:

. . . applies to [another] a condition or requirement which he applies or

would apply equally to persons not of the same racial group as that other
but –
  (i)   which is such that the proportion of persons of the same racial
        group as that other who can comply with it is considerably smaller
        than the proportion of persons not of that racial group who can
        comply with it; and
  (ii) which he cannot show to be justifiable irrespective of the colour,
        race, nationality or ethnic or national origins of the person to
        whom it is applied; and
  (iii) which is to the detriment of that other because he cannot comply
        with it.

'Racial group' means 'a group of persons defined by reference to colour,
race, nationality or ethnic or national origins'.

In *Tower Hamlets London Borough Council* v. *Qayyum* (1987)[7] the
EAT gave some guidance on how tribunals should approach cases of
indirect racial discrimination:

(1) Identify the colour, race, nationality or ethnic origin of the applicant.
(2) Ascertain whether there is a racial group of similar colour, national-
    ity or ethnic origin as the applicant.
(3) It is then necessary to see whether or not there had been a require-
    ment or condition imposed generally, irrespective of race or nation-
    ality or ethnic origin.
(4) It is then necessary to determine whether the proportion of the racial
    group to which the applicant belonged and to which the requirement
    or condition applied was considerably smaller than the comparable
    proportion of the indigenous group.

In *Hussein* v. *Saints Complete House Furnishers* (1979)[8] the employer
told the Job Centre that he did not want to be sent any applicants who
lived in Liverpool 8, because he did not want their unemployed friends
hanging around his shop. This was a requirement: in order to be eligible
for the job, you must not live in Liverpool 8. Yet the proportion of black
people who could comply was considerably smaller than the proportion
of non-black people. Blacks formed 50 per cent of the population of
Liverpool 8 but only 2 per cent of the population of Liverpool as a
whole. Hussein could not comply, and the employer could not justify the
requirement, as he should not have ruled out all Liverpool 8 inhabitants
without interviewing them.

Requirement or condition
It is important to note that only a requirement or condition is unlawful:
preferences and practices which have a discriminatory impact are not
necessarily unlawful. In *Perera* v. *Civil Service Commission (No. 2)*

(1982)[9] a Sri Lankan lawyer had been rejected by the Civil Service Commission. In addition to requiring a qualification as a barrister or solicitor, the selection panel assessed applicants using various criteria: age, practical experience in the UK, ability to communicate in English, and so on. The Court of Appeal held that these were not 'requirements or conditions', as they were not absolute *musts*: an exceptional candidate might still be appointed even though their ability to communicate in English might be poor.

This case was followed in *Meer* v. *London Borough of Tower Hamlets* (1988)[10] where an Indian solicitor had been rejected for a post with Tower Hamlets. Again, a variety of criteria, including experience in Tower Hamlets, were used in drawing up a shortlist, but none of these criteria were 'musts'. The Court of Appeal confirmed that *Perera* was correctly decided, although the judges did recognise that the use of such preferences could have a discriminatory effect in practice. The CRE has frequently expressed its concern about the effect of the *Perera* decision and called on the government to change the law, so far to no avail.

The Commission has pointed out that the practices which have the most effect on ethnic minority recruitment are practices such as 'recruiting wholly by word of mouth, giving preference to children of existing employees for apprenticeships, or only trawling for vacancies internally'. These would not amount to absolute bars to recruitment, and therefore are not unlawful. The CRE has recommended that 'any practice, policy or situation which is continued, allowed or introduced, and which has a significant adverse impact on a particular racial group, and which is not necessary, should be unlawful'.

Employers who are serious about equal opportunities should examine their recruitment preferences and criteria and check for any adverse impact on ethnic minorities. Such preferences may be justifiable, but it is important to weigh up any perceived business-related reasons for applying the criteria against the impact on ethnic minorities: otherwise, the employer may not be getting the best person for the job. It should also be remembered that tribunals will examine any 'preferences' to see whether, in reality, they operate as strict requirements. In addition, if an employer applies a preference or criterion with the *intention* of excluding ethnic minorities, then this will amount to direct racial discrimination.

Proportion who can comply

It is now clear that a person's ability to comply with a requirement or condition means whether they can comply *in practice*, not in some absolute sense. So, for example, anyone could physically comply with a 'no beards' rule, but such a rule may still be indirect discrimination against Sikhs: the test is whether the person can comply in accordance with the customs and traditions of their racial group. So a requirement to wear a particular kind of headgear may be also indirectly discriminatory against Sikhs, if it is not justifiable.[11] Similarly, a requirement that employees work on Saturdays may amount to indirect discrimination against Jews, unless the employer can justify it.

In establishing whether the proportion of a particular racial group who can comply with the requirement or condition is smaller than the proportion of people not of that racial group, it is important to understand that the issue is not one of numbers or ratios (of black to white, for example), but of relative effect. So, for example, a tribunal would examine what proportion of male Sikhs could comply with a 'no beards' rule – 50 per cent – and then compare that with the proportion of male non-Sikhs who could comply – perhaps 95 per cent. If the first proportion is considerably smaller than the second, then there is indirect discrimination (unless, of course, it can be justified).

There is no clear guidance in law as to exactly what 'considerably smaller' means, and tribunals have reached differing decisions on this. The CRE has recommended that a 20 per cent difference should be treated as significant and advises employers to use the 'four-fifths' rule in analysing data produced by ethnic monitoring. If there is a disparity in success rates – for recruitment or promotion etc. – of one-fifth or more, then employers should try to find out why and, if necessary, take steps to deal with it.

Detriment

It is also necessary for the individual to show that they have suffered some detriment: for example, if someone has not personally been excluded from employment because of a 'no beards' rule, then they cannot bring a case on the matter. Detriment in this context means 'putting under a disadvantage'. So failure to get a job or promotion, or a demotion, transfer or dismissal would all amount to a detriment. It is also clear that racial harassment is a detriment. In *De Souza* v. *Automobile Association* (1986)[12] the Court of Appeal ruled that there was a detriment if the reasonable worker had been disadvantaged in the circumstances in which they had to work.

In *Raval* v. *Department of Health and Social Security* (1985)[13] the issue was a requirement that employees had a GCE 'O' level in English Language. The tribunal held that this did not operate to Miss Raval's detriment, because it would be easy for her to take and pass the exam in the future. This seems to miss the point: she could not comply with it in practice and did not get the job, thus it operated to her detriment. Employers would be better advised to ensure that any educational requirements are justifiable, instead of arguing that they were not, in fact, detrimental because the individual could easily obtain them.

Justification

Even if a requirement or condition does have an adverse impact on a particular racial group, the employer may nevertheless be able to justify its
use. Deciding whether it is justifiable involves a balancing act: tribunals
look on the one hand at the discriminatory impact of the requirement or
condition, and on the other hand at the reasonable business needs of the
employer. In *Hampson* v. *Department of Education and Science* (1989)[14]
the Court of Appeal held that tribunals should apply the same test as in
sex discrimination and equal pay cases, based on the ECJ decision in the
Bilka-Kaufhaus case.[15] So the employer must show:

- a real need on the part of the undertaking, and
- that the requirement imposed is appropriate and necessary in order to
  achieve that need.

This is much stricter than the test laid down in *Ojutiku and Oburoni* v.
Manpower Services Commission (1982)[16] where the Court of Appeal
stated that it would be enough if the reasons were 'sound and tolerable to
right-thinking people'. Nevertheless, the cases show that tribunals look
at justification from the employer's perspective. It is also clear that the
question of justifiability is a question of fact for individual industrial tribunals. In *Raval* the EAT said that it was up to the tribunal to find that
the requirement of English 'O' level was justified, 'even though another
tribunal may perfectly reasonably have taken another view'. The difficulty
with such an approach is that it gives no clear guidance to employers
who are keen to avoid discriminatory practices. The CRE has recommended, instead, that employers should be required to show that the
practice having the adverse impact 'is necessary to ensure that the functions of the job are carried out safely and competently and that the same
end cannot be achieved in a less discriminatory manner'.

Discrimination by victimisation

Like section 4 of the SDA 1975, section 2 of the RRA 1976 makes it discriminatory to treat a person less favourably than others because they
have taken certain actions in connection with the RRA. It is unlawful to
treat a person less favourably where the reason for the treatment is that
they have done one of the following acts:

- brought proceedings under the RRA (either against the discriminator
  or any other person)
- given evidence or information in connection with proceedings brought
  by anyone against the discriminator or any other person under the RRA

- otherwise done anything under or by reference to the RRA in relation to the discriminator or any other person
- alleged that the discriminator or any other person has committed an act which would amount to a contravention of the RRA, regardless of whether the allegation specifically states this.

It is also unlawful victimisation if the discriminator victimises the person because they know that the person intends to do any of those acts, or suspects that the person has done or intends to do any of those acts. However, if an individual makes a false allegation and is not acting in good faith, then employers can penalise that individual without contravening the Act.

These provisions are very complex, and have not been very successful in protecting employees from victimisation. It is necessary for the individual to show:

- that they have done an act which falls within one of the four categories. In relation to acts done 'under or by reference to' the RRA 1976, this should be interpreted broadly: it is not necessary that the individual focused his mind specifically on a particular provision of the Act.
- that they have been treated less favourably than other persons in the relevant circumstances. This means that the individual's treatment should be compared with how another employee would have been treated, where the second employee had not done the relevant act.
- that the discriminatory treatment was done because they did a protected act under the race relations legislation. So the employer's motive must be consciously connected with the fact that the employee did an act by reference to the race relations legislation.

The last requirement severely limits the scope of the protection. In *Aziz* v. *Trinity Street Taxis Ltd* (1988)[17] a taxi driver suspected that he was being unfairly treated by a collective organisation of taxi drivers set up to operate a radio control system and that this treatment was racially motivated. He secretly recorded conversations with other taxi drivers, with a view to using these recordings in legal proceedings. When the organisation found out about the tape recordings, they voted to expel him on the ground that this constituted a serious breach of trust. The Court of Appeal held that making the tape recordings was a protected act, as it was done by reference to the RRA 1976 in a broad sense. Mr Aziz had also been treated less favourably than a taxi driver who had not done the protected act. But Mr Aziz's claim failed, because he could not show that the reason why he had been expelled was specifically because he had done an act *connected with the race relations legislation*: the taxi drivers would have expelled any member who made secret tape recordings, whatever the reason. They were not motivated by the fact that the recordings were connected with proceedings under the RRA. This interpretation provides limited protection for those who are victimised for disclosing confidential information that demonstrates that the employer has committed or intends to commit an act of racial discrimination. The CRE has recommended that the Act be amended so that there is protection against a person's suffering any detriment whatsoever as a result of their doing any of the protected acts, regardless of whether the employer was motivated by the fact that the act was related to the race relations legislation. There should clearly be a difference between employees who disclose confidential information in order to prove or establish racial discrimination, and those who disclose such information for other purposes. Employers should take steps to ensure that racially motivated acts, such as harassment, refusal of job or promotion opportunities, or dismissal, are not tolerated, and employees should be encouraged to report any such acts to the employer, rather than the employer treating any such disclosure as a reason for victimising the person who reports it.

Unlawful discrimination in employment

Section 4(1) of the RRA 1976 provides that it is unlawful for an employer to discriminate against a person:

  (a) in the arrangements he makes for the purpose of determining who should be offered that employment; or
  (b) in the terms on which he offers him that employment: or
  (c) by refusing or deliberately omitting to offer him that employment.

Section 4(2) makes it unlawful for an employer to discriminate against an employee:

  (a) in the terms of employment which he affords him; or
  (b) in the way he affords him access to opportunities for promotion, transfer or training, or to any other benefits, facilities or services, or by refusing or deliberately omitting to afford him access to them; or
  (c) by dismissing him, or subjecting him to any other detriment.

Like the SDA 1975, the RRA 1976 covers the self-employed as well as employees, apprentices, contract workers and agency workers. The employment must be at an establishment within Great Britain, and work done wholly or mainly outside Great Britain is excluded. As with the SDA 1975, work on ships, aircraft and hovercraft registered in Great Britain is covered, unless the work is done wholly outside Great Britain.

The Race Relations Act 1976 did not extend to Northern Ireland, but the Government has announced that it intends to introduce legislation similar to the RRA 1976 for Northern Ireland, probably in 1996.

Exclusions

It is lawful to discriminate on racial grounds against job applicants seeking work in a private household. But this exception does not cover discrimination by victimisation.

Seamen recruited abroad are not covered, and there is an exception which allows employers to discriminate on racial grounds in training employees not normally resident in Great Britain where those employees intend to exercise those skills abroad.

Genuine occupational qualifications

Discrimination in recruitment or promotion is permissible in cases where being of a particular racial or ethnic group, or nationality, is a 'genuine occupational qualification' (GOQ). Section 5(2) of the RRA 1976 sets out the only four grounds on which race etc. can amount to a GOQ:

- where the job involves participation in a dramatic performance or other entertainment, and a person of the particular racial group is required for reasons of authenticity
- where the job involves participation as an artist's or photographic model in the production of a work of art or visual image, and a person of a particular racial group is required for reasons of authenticity
- where the job involves working in a place where food and drink is provided to and consumed by members of the public, in a particular setting, and a member of the racial group is required for reasons of authenticity
- where the job involves providing persons of a particular racial group with personal services promoting their welfare, and those services can be most effectively be provided by a person of that racial group.

In *Tottenham Green Under-Fives' Centre* v. *Marshall* (1991)[18] the EAT gave a broad interpretation to this last provision. A playgroup wanted to advertise for an Afro-Caribbean nursery nurse, in order to replace an Afro-Caribbean member of staff who had left. The playgroup had children from a wide variety of ethnic backgrounds and wanted to maintain cultural links with the children's home backgrounds, read and talk to them in dialect, and look after their skin and hair. The EAT held that race was therefore a GOQ, as part of the job involved providing personal services. As long as the duty was not a sham, or so trivial as to be disregarded, then industrial tribunals could not ignore the duty because they felt that it was relatively unimportant compared with other aspects of the job. However, it is important to note that race ceases to be a GOQ if the employer already has employees of the relevant racial group, and:

- those employees are capable of carrying out the duties falling within the exception, and
- it would be reasonable to employ them on those duties, and
- there are enough of those employees to meet the employer's requirements without undue inconvenience.

So if the playgroup already employed Afro-Caribbean nursery nurses, then the GOQ might not have applied.

It is essential that the job holder provides 'personal services'. In *Lambeth London Borough* v. *Commission for Racial Equality* (1990)[19] the Council advertised for housing managers, restricting applicants to those of Asian or Afro-Caribbean origin. They sought to justify this on the ground that a large proportion of people housed by the Council belonged to those groups. The Court of Appeal held that this did not fall within the exception. 'Personal services' involves some face-to-face contact between the job holder and the recipient of those services: it is not enough that a service is provided which ultimately affects an individual. The Court of Appeal also stressed that the RRA 1976 should not be interpreted as promoting positive action: the main aim of the Act is to outlaw racial discrimination, and the GOQ exceptions cannot be interpreted so as to allow employers to achieve a racially balanced team.

The employer does not have to show that the personal services could *only* be provided by someone from the particular racial group: it is enough that they can '*most effectively*' be provided by such a person. In the *Lambeth* case it was said that 'where language or a knowledge and understanding of cultural and religious background are of importance, then those services may be most effectively provided by a person of a particular racial group'.

Recruitment methods

Advertisements

The CRE, like the EOC, has issued a Code of Practice which contains useful guidance on recruitment practices. The Code recommends that employers should not recruit through the recommendations of existing employees in situations where the workforce concerned is predominantly of one racial group but the labour market is multi-racial. Nor should employers rely on procedures whereby applicants are mainly or wholly supplied through trade unions. Although such practices may not be strictly illegal (in that they do not operate as absolute bars to recruitment), it is clear that informal recruitment methods, such as relying on word of mouth, advertising vacancies internally, relying on unsolicited application letters, or using headhunters, tend to reproduce the existing ethnic make-up of the workforce. Formal, external advertisements are preferable. The Code recommends that employers:

> should not confine advertisements unjustifiably to those areas or publications which would exclude or disproportionately reduce the number of applicants of a particular racial group.

Employers who are committed to equal opportunities can go further and take steps to encourage applications from ethnic minorities. The Code recommends that employers state in advertisements and job literature that they are equal opportunities employers. Employers should also consider advertising job vacancies in the ethnic minority press, using images of ethnic minorities in job advertisements and promotional material, translating advertisements into ethnic minority languages and circulating job vacancies to ethnic minority organisations. In addition, section 38 of the RRA 1976 provides that, if a racial group has been under-represented or unrepresented in a particular kind of work at the establishment within the last 12 months, then an employer can specifically state that applications are encouraged from members of that racial group. Evidence suggests that, where the relevant statutory section is mentioned in the advertisement, there are fewer complaints. Discrimination at the point of selection is, however, unlawful.

It is also unlawful to publish an advertisement which indicates, or might reasonably be understood to indicate, an intention to discriminate, except where race is a GOQ. Even though it is lawful to discriminate on racial grounds for a job in a private household, it is still unlawful to publish an advertisement showing an intention to so discriminate: so an advertisement for a white nanny will be unlawful.

Selection procedures

Employers must take care to ensure that selection procedures do not have a racially discriminatory impact. There is considerable evidence of direct racial discrimination in recruitment processes, whereby candidates with foreign sounding names, or who live in areas of a town or city with a large immigrant population, are not asked for interview. This is unlawful direct racial discrimination, although it can be difficult to prove before a tribunal. In *Thiruppathy* v. *Steggles Palmer* (1991)[20] Ms Thiruppathy applied for articles with a firm of solicitors and was rejected without interview. She then sent in an application in the name of 'Jane Thorpe' and was invited for interview. She made a complaint of racial discrimination, and the tribunal found that one in three white applicants had been called for interview, compared with one in six ethnic minority candidates. The firm was found to have discriminated on racial grounds. However, in the absence of such evidence, many candidates will be unable to prove discrimination.

Employers who are committed to equal opportunities will follow the recommendations of the CRE and engage in ethnic monitoring of job applicants. The CRE recommends that employers use the nine categories used in the 1991 census. These are:

White
Black – African
Black – Caribbean
Black – Other (please specify)
Indian
Pakistani
Bangladeshi
Chinese
Other – (please specify)

The CRE recommends that this information should be requested in the application form itself, as there is a higher response rate, and they concluded that there was no evidence that this prejudiced employers to reject people on racial grounds. However, many employers ask for such information, together with questions on sex, marital status and disability, on a separate piece of paper, with a clear statement to applicants that the information is for monitoring purposes only and will not be passed on to selection panels. In *Dillistone* v. *London Borough of Lambeth* (1992)[21] an internal applicant for a post objected to the questions on the application form concerning his race, gender and marital status. He refused to answer the questions and instead wrote: 'The concept of racial grouping serves to endorse divisions and is therefore irreconcilable with the spirit and tenets of equal opportunities, whose principles it negates. If information is sought for monitoring purposes, its place lies elsewhere.' Mr Dillistone was not short-listed for the job, because, according to the Council, his answer showed that he was not committed to Lambeth's equal opportunities policy and therefore would be unable to function effectively in the job he had applied for. The EAT held that Mr Dillistone had not been discriminated against on the ground of race.

Application forms should be kept as clear and simple as possible. The

CRE Code of Practice states that, in particular, firms should not reject candidates simply because they are unable to complete application forms unassisted, unless 'personal completion of the form is a valid test of the standard of English required for safe and effective performance of the job'.

In determining the job description and person specification, employers should be careful not to require higher levels of educational attainment than are necessary for the job in question, or to only consider candidates with UK qualifications, or to require specific patterns of previous experience, as all these can have an indirectly discriminatory effect. The use of selection tests should also be carefully considered, as they may contain 'irrelevant questions or exercises on matters which may be unfamiliar to racial minority applicants . . . for example, general knowledge questions on matters more likely to be familiar to indigenous applicants'. The CRE recommends that selection tests be geared to measuring an individual's ability to do, or train for, the job in question. Nevertheless, a well-designed and validated selection test may help to eliminate racial discrimination from the selection process.

At interview, care should be taken to ensure that candidates are not asked questions which could lead to inferences of discrimination. It may be necessary to ask about qualifications or experience gained overseas, but this should not be done in a way that may make it appear that the qualifications or experience are being undervalued. It may be discriminatory to ask candidates questions about time off for religious observance, or whether they will want extended leave to visit family overseas. However, in *Dhatt* v. *McDonalds Hamburgers Ltd* (1991)[22] the Court of Appeal ruled that it was lawful for an employer to ask a candidate to produce evidence that they had a work permit.

Employers should ensure that adequate records are kept for each step of the selection process, as this will be relevant if any unsuccessful applicant does bring a discrimination claim. It is important for the employer to be able to show that each candidate was measured against the job description and person specification, and so the reasons for rejecting unsuccessful candidates must be recorded, as well as the reasons for selecting the successful candidate. It is therefore important that adequate notes are taken at every stage of the selection process. Tribunals are also paying increasing attention to the employer's equal opportunity policy and measuring what actually happened against the procedures laid down by the policy. Failure to follow one's own procedures can raise an inference of discrimination.

Under the RRA 1976 and the SDA 1975, an individual who has brought or is considering bringing a complaint can send the employer a list of questions, and if the employer fails to reply, or is equivocal or evasive, then the tribunal can draw an adverse inference. Tribunals will

also order the discovery of documents – an order that the employer disclose relevant documents in their possession. Employees have used these
procedures to get details of all applicants for jobs, and successful applicants for those jobs, over a period of time. In *West Midlands Passenger
Transport Executive* v. *Singh* (1988)[23] the Court of Appeal ordered the
employer to disclose details of all job applicants over the past two years.

Using recruitment services

Many employers recruit staff through recruitment agencies. Section 14 of
the RRA 1976 makes it unlawful for employment agencies to discriminate on the ground of race 'in the terms on which an agency offers to
provide any of its services, or by refusing or deliberately omitting to provide any of its services, or in the way it provides any of its services'. It is
also unlawful, under sections 30 and 31, to instruct or put pressure on
someone else to discriminate. In *CRE* v. *Gibson Funeral Services*
(1992)[24] the employer telephoned the local Job Centre to advertise a
vacancy, but told them that he did not want to be sent 'any of our
coloured friends'. When pressed by the Job Centre, he told them that
there was no way that he would employ a Pakistani. The matter was
referred to the CRE and, after attempts to resolve the matter informally
failed, the CRE took proceedings. The employer was found liable for
attempting to instruct or induce the Job Centre to discriminate against
Pakistanis.

Discriminatory terms of employment

It is unlawful to offer employment on terms which discriminate on racial
grounds, whether or not the offer is accepted. So it would be unlawful
for an employer to offer ethnic minorities employment on lower pay than
whites, or only to offer jobs on the night shift to ethnic minorities.

Once a person is employed, it is unlawful for the employer to discriminate in the terms of employment which they afford that person. In 1993,
John Haggas plc, a mill in West Yorkshire, was found to have discriminated against Asian night-shift workers. The night shift was all-Asian and
had been threatened with dismissal if they refused to take on extra duties,
whereas this had not happened to the all-white day shift. The tribunal also
found that the Asian workers were not paid overtime, received four days'
less holiday a year than the white workers, and had no chance of promotion. Forty-nine workers were awarded £4,000 compensation each.[25]

It is sometimes alleged that employers discriminate indirectly when
they insist on certain hours of work which coincide with religious observance. In *Ahmad* v. *ILEA* (1977)[26] a Muslim schoolteacher resigned from

his job because his employers refused to let him take an extra 45 minutes' lunch break on a Friday in order to attend the mosque. The majority of the Court of Appeal held that this was not unlawful under the Education Act 1944. If Mr Ahmad had brought his case under the RRA 1976, he would have had to have shown that the proportion of his racial group (as Muslims are not themselves a racial group) who could comply with the requirement or condition was considerably smaller than those not of his racial group. Assuming he could have shown this, the key issue would then have been whether the employer could justify the requirement.

Similar issues arise in relation to orthodox Jews, who cannot work on Friday evenings and Saturdays. The Metropolitan Police reached a settlement with a police constable who complained that he could not comply with the shift rotas. However, in *Wetstein* v. *Misprestige Management Services Ltd* (1993)[27] Ms Wetstein registered with an employment agency, but the agency refused to offer her any work because she could not work a full Friday during the winter. The EAT upheld an industrial tribunal's finding that this was not indirect discrimination. The reasoning was that only between 5 per cent and 10 per cent of Jews are strict Sabbath observers, and so 90 per cent to 95 per cent of Jews could comply with a requirement to work on Friday afternoons. This was not considerably smaller than the proportion of non-Jews who could comply.

Issues have also arisen about dress codes, particularly in relations to Sikhs. In *Singh* v. *Rowntree Mackintosh Ltd* (1979)[28] the employers did not allow beards, and Mr Singh was refused a job because he refused to shave his beard off. The EAT held that the 'no beards' rule was justifiable on hygiene grounds. In *Panesar* v. *Nestlé* (1980)[29] the Court of Appeal upheld a 'no beards' rule in a chocolate factory for the same reason. However, the Employment Act 1989 provides that Sikhs working on construction sites are exempted from the statutory requirement to wear a safety helmet. It is expressly provided that it is not racial discrimination to insist that non-Sikhs continue to wear helmets.

The CRE Code of Practice recommends that where 'employees have particular religious and cultural needs which conflict with existing work requirements, it is recommended that employers should consider whether it is reasonably practicable to vary or adapt these requirements to enable such needs to be met'. The Code also refers to the possibility of employers granting extended leave for employees visiting relatives overseas: 'Many employers have policies which allow annual leave entitlement to be accumulated, or extra unpaid leave to be taken to meet these circumstances. Employers should take care to apply these policies consistently and without unlawful discrimination.' Some employers who give extended leave have had difficulty ensuring that employees return to work on the appointed date, frequently because of visa problems. Employers are entitled to treat this as a disciplinary offence in the ordinary way and should observe the appropriate procedural steps before taking any disciplinary action. Some employers ask employees to sign documents before they leave stating that, in the event of a failure to return on the given date, the employee will be taken to have resigned, or to have dismissed themselves. These documents are unlikely to be upheld by tribunals, who view them as an attempt to contract out of the statutory protection against unfair dismissal. The employer has dismissed the employee in these circumstances, and the tribunal will go on to examine whether or not it was fair.

Promotion and training

It is unlawful for an employer to discriminate in the way he affords employees access to opportunities for promotion, transfer or training. Many of the issues concerning recruitment apply in the same way here. In 1990, the CRE carried out an investigation into promotion procedures at London Underground and found that they operated in a way which discriminated against ethnic minority staff. None of the 63 senior managers recently appointed had been from an ethnic minority; vacancies were not advertised internally or externally; and candidates for promotion were selected on the recommendation of their superiors. The employer could have used the provisions of section 38 of the RRA 1976 to actively encourage employees to apply for promotion.

Section 38 allows positive discrimination on the ground of race in very limited circumstances. Like the equivalent provisions in the SDA 1975, it allows employers to provide training facilities for employees of a particular racial group if they have been unrepresented, or under-represented, in a particular job in the previous 12 months. Similarly, employers can encourage members of a particular racial group to apply for such jobs. However, positive discrimination at the point of selection is always unlawful: an employer can only assist an applicant with training so that they are in a better position to be considered for the job.

One problem that can arise is that ethnic minority employees are concentrated in particular jobs. Here, employers should take care to examine the criteria used for transfer into other areas of work, to ensure that they are not operating in a discriminatory way.

'Some other detriment'

It is unlawful for an employer to subject employees to 'some other detriment'. A detriment simply means being put at a disadvantage. It is not necessary for the employee to show that they have been penalised in some employment-related way; it is enough that a reasonable employee could justifiably complain about their working conditions, even though the conditions were not so bad as to lead the employee to resign. In this context, racial harassment at work is a key issue.

Racial harassment

Racial harassment at work has received less attention than the comparable issue of sexual harassment, but it is nevertheless clear that it is a significant problem. The CRE reported a 27 per cent increase in complaints of racial harassment in 1991–92, and there have been a number of well publicised cases which show that racial harassment counts as racial discrimination. An employee who suffers racial harassment may chose to resign and bring a constructive dismissal claim, assuming that they have two years' continuous employment. Alternatively, an employee may use the RRA 1976, by showing that they have been subjected to 'some other detriment' on racial grounds.

In *De Souza* v. *Automobile Association* (1985)[30] Mrs De Souza was a secretary, who overheard one manager say to another to 'get his typing done by the wog'. She complained of unlawful race discrimination. The Court of Appeal held that racial abuse or racial harassment could amount to a detriment, if a reasonable employee could justifiably complain about their working conditions or working environment. However, an overheard racial insult did not amount to a detriment in these circumstances, as there was no evidence that Mrs De Souza was intended to hear the remark, or that the manager knew or ought reasonably to have known that the remark would get back to her in some way.

However, in many cases the racial abuse is directed towards the complainant, or the words are spoken in their presence, and it is clear that tribunals view this as unlawful harassment. In *Sutton* v. *Balfour Beatty Construction* (1992)[31] a tribunal disagreed with the employer that the term 'black bastards' was one of camaraderie. In *Mann* v. *Moody* (1993)[32] a Department of Social Security line manager made a lighthearted reference to 'Paki shops' in the presence of an Asian employee. This was held to constitute racial discrimination: 'Paki' was a racially abusive term, and the manager ought reasonably to have been aware that Ms Mann would overhear it and find it offensive. The fact that Ms Mann may have been sensitive about race discrimination was a reason for taking more care, not a defence. This highlights the fact that racial harassment, like sexual harassment, is defined subjectively: the issue is whether the conduct or language is offensive to the recipient, not the 'reasonable' employee.

A crucial issue in many racial harassment cases is the extent to which the employer is liable for the acts of their employees. Section 32(1) provides that:

> Anything done by a person in the course of his employment shall be treated for the purposes of this Act as done by his employer as well as by him, whether or not it was done with the employer's knowledge or approval.

So ignorance of the harassment is no defence. However, it is not always clear that acts of racial abuse and harassment are done 'in the course of [the harasser's] employment'. In *Tower Boot Co Ltd* v. *Jones* (1995)[33] Mr Jones was subjected to serious racial abuse by his fellow employees: he was called names, had metal bolts thrown at his head, and was branded with a hot screwdriver. The EAT ruled that these acts were not 'in the course of employment'. The phrase has a well-established meaning in law, developed in the law of negligence which draws a distinction between actions that fall outside the course of employment and actions that are improper or unauthorised modes of doing what the employee was employed to do. The EAT held by a majority that actions such as branding someone with a hot screwdriver could not by any stretch of the imagination be described as an improper mode of performing authorised tasks. This decision can be criticised for taking too narrow a view of what 'the course of employment' involves, and the minority member gave a strong dissent, arguing that it is inappropriate to apply the very strict principles of vicarious liability developed in the law of tort to cases of racial discrimination. This approach is supported by the Code of Practice issued by the CRE.

The employer will have a defence if it can be shown that 'he took such steps as were reasonably practicable to prevent the employee from doing that act, or from doing in the course of his employment acts of that description'. It is clear that the best way for an employer to do this is to establish a policy to prevent racial harassment. As with sexual harassment policies, this should consist of a clear statement of what racial harassment is, that it is unacceptable in the organisation, and what the procedures are to deal with harassment. These latter will usually involve the training of staff and managers, informal procedures designed to stop harassment, and then formal disciplinary procedures, if necessary. Relatively few employers have separate racial harassment policies. Although a general policy on harassment at work is better than no policy at all, employers would be well advised to highlight racial harassment, with examples of unacceptable conduct, in any general policy. Attention should also be given to training in racial issues: in *Mann* the DSS was criticised by the tribunal for failing to train its employees in racial awareness. The tribunal took the view that no properly trained manager would have made such a remark, even on a jocular basis.

The CRE have issued guidance for employers on the legal implications of racial harassment[34] and how best to combat it. The guidance offers detailed advice on the implementation of a racial harassment policy.

The Criminal Justice and Public Order Act 1994 created a new criminal offence of intentional harassment. A person is guilty of the offence if, with intent, he or she causes another person harassment, alarm or distress by

- using threatening, abusive or insulting words or behaviour, or disorderly behaviour
- displaying any writing, sign or other visible representation which is threatening, abusive or insulting.

It is a defence for the accused to show that their conduct was reasonable in all the circumstances.

This offence was introduced primarily to deal with racial harassment, but is wide enough to cover sexual harassment, as well as harassment on grounds such as sexuality, age or disability. Employers should examine their harassment policies to take this new offence, in force since 3 February 1995, into account.

Remedies

There is no longer any limit on the amount of compensation that can be awarded by tribunals in race discrimination cases following the Race Relations Remedies Act 1994.

Key points

- Direct and indirect racial discrimination is unlawful.
- Direct discrimination involves less favourable treatment on racial grounds.
- Racial grounds covers colour, race, nationality, ethnic or national origin.
- Ethnic groups include Jews, Sikhs, and gypsies, but not Rastafarians or Muslims. However, discrimination against the latter may amount to indirect racial discrimination.
- Indirect discrimination involves applying a neutral requirement or condition which has a disproportionate impact on members of a racial group and which the employer cannot justify.
- Victimisation involves treating an individual less favourably because

they have taken certain action in connection with the RRA 1976. It is unlawful.

- Employers should check recruitment procedures for direct and indirect discrimination.
- Employers should advertise jobs in publications likely to reach ethnic minorities. Word-of-mouth recruitment should be avoided.
- Employers should keep records of the ethnic origins of job applicants and applicants for promotion.
- Consideration should be given to special encouragement or training where ethnic minorities are under-represented.
- Employers should check that qualifications required for jobs are necessary.
- Selection tests should be examined for possible racial bias.
- Records should be kept at every stage of the selection and promotion process.
- Recruitment services should not be given any instructions to discriminate on racial grounds.
- Employers should endeavour to allow employees time off for religious observance.
- Employers should ensure that ethnic minorities are encouraged to apply for promotion.
- Employers should consider introducing a specific racial harassment policy.

References

1 [1980] IRLR 142
2 [1985] IRLR 426
3 [1983] IRLR 209
4 *Commission for Racial Equality* v. *Dutton* [1989] IRLR 8
5 *Dawkins* v. *Department of the Environment* [1983] IRLR 284
6 [1978] IRLR 532
7 [1987] ICR 729
8 [1979] IRLR 337
9 [1982] IRLR 147
10 [1988] IRLR 399
11 Note that the Employment Act 1989 allows Sikhs working on building sites to exempt themselves from the general requirement to wear safety helmets.
12 [1986] IRLR 103
13 [1985] IRLR 370
14 [1989] IRLR 69
15 See Chapter 2, p. 9

16 [1982] IRLR 418
17 [1988] IRLR 204
18 [1991] IRLR 162
19 [1990] IRLR 231
20 See IRLB 476, p. 7
21 See IRLB 481, p. 11
22 [1991] IRLR 130
23 [1988] IRLR 186
24 See EOR-DCLD No. 15, p. 8
25 See the *Guardian*, 29.5.93
26 [1977] ICR 490
27 Unreported, 19.3.93. See IRLB 482, p. 15
28 [1979] IRLR 199
29 [1980] IRLR 64
30 [1985] IRLR 87
31 See EOR-DCLD, No. 12
32 See EOR-DCLD, No. 15
33 [1995] IRLR 529
34 *Racial Harassment at Work: What employers can do about it*, CRE,
    1995

Chapter 8
Religious discrimination

There is no specific legal prohibition against discrimination on the ground of religious belief in Great Britain, although such discrimination is unlawful in Northern Ireland. However, employers need to be aware that discrimination on the ground of religious belief, either intentional or unintentional, can amount to unlawful indirect discrimination on the ground of race.

As was seen in Chapter 7, the Race Relations Act 1976 only prohibits discrimination on the grounds of 'colour, race, nationality, ethnic or national origin'. An ethnic group was defined by the House of Lords in *Mandla* v. *Dowell Lee* (1983)[1] as having two essential characteristics:

- a long shared history, of which the group is conscious as distinguishing it from other groups, and the memory of which it keeps alive
- a cultural tradition of its own, including family and social customs and manners often, but not necessarily, involved with religious observance.

So Sikhs were held to be an ethnic group, as are Jews, but not Muslims or Rastafarians.

However, an employer's conscious decision to discriminate against Muslims or Rastafarians would probably amount to indirect racial discrimination. For example, if an employer advertised a job, but made it clear that no Rastafarian would be considered for the position, then they would be applying a requirement or condition that, in order to be eligible for the job, it would be necessary not to be a Rastafarian. If an unsuccessful applicant was of Afro-Caribbean origin, then they may be able to show that the proportion of people of Afro-Caribbean origin who could comply with the requirement of not being a Rastafarian was considerably smaller than the proportion of people not of that racial group. The key issue would then be whether the employer could justify the requirement – i.e. show some business-related reason for not employing Rastafarians in that particular job.

In practice, problems are more likely to arise because the employer requires people to work at times that are incompatible with religious observance. So, for example, Muslims may require time off at certain times of the year to attend the mosque, and orthodox Jews are unable to work on Friday evenings or Saturdays. To demand that people work at such times may be indirect racial discrimination. However, in *Wetstein* v. *Misprestige Management Services Ltd* (1993)[2] the EAT held that a requirement to work Friday evenings was not indirect racial discrimination, as the proportion of Jews who could comply with the requirement was found to be 90–95 per cent. Since this was not significantly different from the proportion of non-Jews who could comply, there was no indirect discrimination.

Nevertheless, it is suggested that employers should endeavour to be flexible about such matters and to accommodate their employees' religious observance whenever possible. Similar issues may arise in the future in relation to Sunday working. The EC Directive on Working Time, which has not yet been finalised, proposes that, in principle, employees should be entitled to Sunday off, and it seems likely that, whatever proposals the Government finally introduces on Sunday shop opening, there will be provision for employees with religious (or indeed any other) objection to working on Sundays to be protected from dismissal or unfavourable treatment.

Northern Ireland

Religious discrimination is clearly a problem in Northern Ireland, and since 1976 religious and political discrimination has been unlawful there. However, the Government recognised that the original legislation had done little to improve employment prospects for the Catholic minority, and introduced the Fair Employment (Northern Ireland) Act 1989.

The Act prohibits discrimination in employment on the grounds of religious belief or political opinion. Both direct and indirect discrimination are outlawed, and individuals can complain to a Fair Employment Tribunal. In addition, a Fair Employment Commission was established. All employers who employ more than 10 employees must register with the Commission and file annual returns on the religious composition of their workforce. In addition, employers with more than 250 employees are required to submit returns on applicants for jobs. Registered employers must review their employment law practices every three years and assess what further action, if any, should be taken in order to promote fair employment. The Commission can require undertakings and issue directions, and set goals and timetables for employers to meet. The Tribunal has enforcement powers in respect of these undertakings or directions. There is also a limited form of 'contract compliance', in that any employer who fails to comply with the monitoring or registration requirements, or who fails to observe a Tribunal order, will not normally be eligible for public contracts put out to tender.

In many ways, the Fair Employment (Northern Ireland) Act 1989 is a considerable improvement, in terms of equal opportunities policy and practice, on the Sex Discrimination Act 1975 and the Race Relations Act 1976. Employers have a legal obligation to undertake monitoring. It remains to be seen how successful the Act is in reducing religious discrimination in Northern Ireland, but it is tempting to conclude that the Government takes the problem more seriously than sex and race discrimination. As with sex and race discrimination, there is no longer any limit on the amount of compensation that a tribunal can award.

Key points

- Religious discrimination is not of itself unlawful, but may amount to indirect racial discrimination.
- Employers should try to accommodate the religious practices of their employees whenever possible.
- Employers in Northern Ireland cannot discriminate on the grounds of religious belief or political opinion and must undertake workforce monitoring and conduct reviews of their employment policies.

References

1 [1983] IRLR 209
2 Unreported, 19.3.93. See IRLB 482, p. 15

Chapter 9
Age discrimination

Age discrimination appears to be very common in Britain, despite an increasing perception that older workers are under-used and under-valued. A recent survey by the Equal Opportunities Review (EOR)[1] found that one out of four advertisements specified that applicants should be under 45, with around half giving an age limit of 35 or under. As well as age discrimination in recruitment, employers discriminate against older existing employees in terms of training and promotion. Discrimination in job advertisements is far more widespread in the private sector than in the public sector, but a detailed survey of employment practices in local authorities showed that, in practice, there was considerable bias against older workers.

It is not, in itself, unlawful to discriminate in employment on the ground of age. However, it is possible that age discrimination is an indirect form of sex or race discrimination. So in *Price* v. *Civil Service Commission* (1977)[2] job applicants had to be between 17 and 28. It was held that this was a requirement or condition and that a smaller proportion of otherwise suitably qualified women could comply with the requirement in practice than the proportion of men who could comply, because of women's child-rearing responsibilities. Nor could the employer justify the requirement.

However, it is not easy to successfully claim indirect discrimination based on age:

- First, the employee must show that the age limit was an absolute bar, rather than simply a preference on behalf of the employer for employees under a particular age.
- Secondly, the employee has to show that the proportion of people of a particular sex or racial group who can comply with the requirement or condition is considerably smaller than the proportion of people of the opposite sex or not of that racial group who can comply.

In *Jones* v. *University of Manchester* (1993)[3] the University advertised for a careers adviser, 'preferably aged between 27–35 years', a graduate, and with a record of successful experience. Miss Jones was 46 and was not short-listed. She argued that this was indirect discrimination against women mature students. The Court of Appeal refused to interfere with the decision of the industrial tribunal that, although the age limit was expressed as a preference, it was in fact an absolute barrier. In any event, the Court of Appeal held that the employer could justify the requirement. One of the judges, Lord Justice Evans, commented that 'I cannot help feeling that this is essentially a case about discrimination by age . . . and it is unsurprising that attempts to convert it into a case of indirect sex discrimination should meet obstacles which are difficult, and in the present case on the evidence given, impossible for the applicant to overcome.'

Similar difficulties will apply to an applicant who tries to bring a case of indirect discrimination on the ground of race – although in *Perera* v. *Civil Service Commission (No.2)* (1982)[4] the Employment Appeal Tribunal (EAT) held that an age limit of 32 for posts as a lawyer in the Civil Service was one that a smaller proportion of black people than white people could meet, because of adult immigration to the UK. However, as adult immigration has become more difficult, such an argument will be less likely to succeed in the future; and, in any case, employers will frequently be able to justify age limits.

Nor does the EC hold out much hope for older workers. A report drawn up by Eurolink Age in 1993 (ironically the European Year of Older People.) demonstrated that the EC, when recruiting staff, generally imposes an upper age limit of 35. The Community institutions justify this on the ground that it is necessary in order to provide individuals with a sufficiently long career structure.

However, research also demonstrates that many employers recognise and value the skills and qualities of older workers. A survey of IPM members found that workers over 40 were seen as more reliable, conscientious and loyal, with better interpersonal skills. The EOR study found that older workers had lower rates of absenteeism and were less likely to change jobs than younger workers. The Government has also taken steps recently to encourage employers to use the skills of older workers more effectively, setting up an Advisory Group on Older Workers to encourage employers not to discriminate in terms of recruitment and training. However, the Government has set its face against legislation, preferring instead a process of information and persuasion.

Although the law does not, in itself, guarantee an end to discrimination, it is nevertheless doubtful whether persuasion alone, without any legal 'teeth' will be enough to eliminate age discrimination. It appears to be one of the most pervasive and accepted forms of employment discrimination, yet is one which will affect everyone (or almost everyone) at some stage in their life. It must be stressed that it is in the employer's interest not to discriminate on the ground of age, as this means that prejudiced attitudes prevent the best person getting the job, or the promotion, or the training opportunity. Employers should consider removing express age limits from jobs and ensuring that staff involved in recruitment and selection do not retain unarticulated assumptions about the age profile of the ideal candidate. Application forms do not need to ask for the candidate's age; this information, like racial origin and marital status, could be collected on a separate form for monitoring purposes. Age discrimination should be part of any equal opportunities policy, and appropriate training should be given. Employers should also ensure that older workers are not overlooked for training courses on the basis of a stereotyped assumption that they cannot adapt to new technology or new ways of working.

Key points

- Avoid age limits in job advertisements wherever possible.
- Check any age limits for possible indirect race or sex discrimination.
- Ensure that older employees are given opportunities for training and promotion.
- Ensure that application forms do not ask for date of birth, or age.
- Raise awareness about age discrimination within the organisation.

References

1 'Age Discrimination – no change!', EOR No. 48, March/April 1993
2 [1977] 1 WLR 1417
3 [1993] IRLR 218
4 [1982] IRLR 147

Chapter 10
Discrimination on grounds of disability

It is clear that disabled people suffer considerable discrimination in employment, both in terms of recruitment into the labour market, and in terms of the lack of promotion and training opportunities once employed.

Part of the problem with tackling the issue of disability at work is that, unlike sex or race discrimination, it is generally accepted that disability can, indeed, impair an individual's suitability for employment. But whilst it would clearly be inappropriate to employ a blind person as a driver, in many if not the majority of cases, disabled employees may be perfectly able to do a wide range of jobs. In particular, if employers were required to make certain adaptations, or provide certain additional facilities, then many more jobs would become accessible to workers with a wide range of disabilities. The Government has finally recognised that the policy of encouraging employers to develop good employment practices with regard to the disabled has been ineffective at tackling the problem, and therefore introduced the Disability Discrimination Bill 1995. The Bill will introduce a right not to be discriminated against in employment and in the provision of goods and services.

Disability and the quota

Before the introduction of the Bill, the major legislative provision concerning disability at work was the Disabled Persons (Employment) Act 1944 (DP(E)A), as amended by the Disabled Persons (Employment) Act 1958. This introduced the quota system. The Act was designed to ensure that 3 per cent of any workforce would be people who were registered as disabled. The Act does not apply to Government Departments or the National Health Service, but these employers have undertaken to comply with the quota provisions.

The Act operates by making it a criminal offence for an employer of 20 or more people to offer a job to someone who is not registered as disabled, unless the employer already employs enough registered disabled employees to meet the 3 per cent quota. In addition, it is a criminal offence to dismiss an employee who is registered as disabled, if the effect of the dismissal would be to reduce the percentage of registered disabled employees to below 3 per cent. This is in addition to the general unfair dismissal provisions. Employers who commit these offences can be fined up to £400 (£2,000 if the employer is a company) and/or imprisoned for three months.

It is generally agreed that the quota system has been a failure. This is partly explained by the reluctance of disabled workers to register; the register has fallen from 936,000 in 1950 to 389,272 in 1986. It is estimated that some 734,000 people are eligible for registration – just over 3 per cent of the workforce. At existing levels of registration, it is a mathematical impossibility for all employers to comply, although many employers do, in fact, have people on their payroll who could register as disabled, such as those with heart disease or diabetes, but who are unwilling to do so. Nor has there been a pattern of enforcement: evidence given to a House of Commons Select Committee in 1990/1991 by Mencap showed that there had been ten prosecutions, seven of which led to fines, the average fine being £62. The decision to prosecute is taken by the Secretary of State for Employment. In 1992, a registered disabled employee who was dismissed from her job sought a judicial review of the Employment Secretary's refusal to prosecute her employer, on the ground that the Minister failed to give any reasons for his decision. As a result, the Minister provided the reasons. He denied that there was a policy of non-enforcement, but stated that officials would first attempt to settle any case by negotiation. If that failed, then prosecution would be considered, in the light of all the evidence, including whether the employer had a defence that the dismissal was reasonable. Here, the conclusion was that the dismissal was reasonable.[2] The quota system is to be abolished when the Disability Discrimination Bill comes into force.

The Disability Discrimination Bill[3]

The Disability Discrimination Bill will introduce for the first time a legal right for disabled people not to be discriminated against in employment. However, the Bill does not follow the same model as the legislation against sex and race discrimination. In particular, the Bill does not use the concepts of direct and indirect discrimination, but rather provides that employers may in certain circumstances be able to justify discriminating against disabled people. However, employers will be required to make reasonable adjustments to the working environment. The Bill also gives disabled people a new right of access to goods, facilities and services, and will require positive action by the providers of such services where this is reasonable and readily achievable.

The Bill defines a disabled person as 'one who has a physical or mental impairment which has a substantial and long-term adverse affect on his or her ability to carry out normal day to day activities'.

- Mental impairment includes mental illnesses or disorders only if they are clinically recognised conditions.
- An impairment has a long-term effect if it has lasted, or can reasonably be expected to last, for at least 12 months or is likely to recur.
- An impairment that consists of severe disfigurement is to be treated as having a substantial effect on the ability of the person to carry out day-to-day activities.
- An impairment is to be taken to affect day-to-day activities only if it affects
  - mobility
  - manual dexterity
  - physical co-ordination
  - continence
  - ability to lift, carry or move everyday objects
  - speech, hearing or eyesight
  - memory or ability to understand
  - perception or risk of physical danger
  - ability to concentrate.

- People whose disability is controlled or corrected by medication or prosthesis will continue to be treated as disabled.
- All those registered as disabled, both on 12 January 1995 and the date on which the Bill comes into force, will be deemed to be disabled for three years.
- People with progressive conditions will be covered.
- Those with a history of disability will be covered.
- The Government has announced that the Bill will be amended in the Commons so as to include people with AIDS or symptomatic HIV within the definition of disability.

There is a new right not to be discriminated against in relation to recruitment, terms and conditions of employment, access to training, promotion or other benefits, dismissal or by subjecting the person to any other detriment. This will apply to employees, applicants, apprentices, people who contract personally to provide services and to protect those working for an employment agency from discrimination by the hirer. An employer discriminates against a disabled person if

- for a reason that relates to the disabled person's ability, he treats him less favourably than he treats or would treat others who do not have the disability
- the employer cannot show that the treatment is justified.

The justification defence will be available 'if, but only if, the reason for the failure is both material to the circumstances of the particular case and substantial'. Regulations may be issued to provide for circumstances in which treatment is taken to be justified, or not justified. However, employers will be under a limited duty to make reasonable adjustments to working arrangements, or any physical features of the workplace, where the existing arrangements or premises place the disabled person at a substantial disadvantage compared with non-disabled people. The Bill gives examples of steps an employer may have to take, including:

- making adjustments to premises
- altering working hours
- assigning the disabled person to a different place of work
- allocating some of his or her duties to another person
- transferring him or her to fill an existing vacancy
- allowing him or her time off for rehabilitation, assessment or training
- giving him or her training
- acquiring or modifying equipment
- modifying instructions or reference manuals
- modifying procedures for assessment or training
- providing a reader or interpreter
- providing supervision

More detailed regulations will be issued, but the Bill states that in deciding whether or not it is reasonable for an employer to take a particular step, regard shall be had to the following:

- the extent to which taking the step would prevent the effect in question
- the extent to which it is practicable for the employer to take the step
- the financial and other costs to the employer and the extent to which it would disrupt any of his activities
- the extent of the employer's financial and other resources
- the availability to the employer of financial or other assistance

Small employers (under 20 employees) are excluded from the requirements of the Bill, although this can be changed by statutory order.

Enforcement will be via tribunals, remedies available including unlimited damages. There will be a time limit of three months for bringing a complaint. The Secretary of State will have power to issue a Code of Practice containing guidance on the new law and encouraging good practice. The Bill also provides for the setting up of a National Disability Council, but this will not have the same powers as the CRE and EOC in relation to enforcement and providing legal assistance with individual claims.

Company reports

The Companies (Directors' Reports) (Employment of Disabled Persons) Regulations 1980 require that, where a company employs more than 250 people, the annual directors' report must contain a statement stating what measures the company has taken during the year:

- to give full and fair consideration to job applications by disabled people, having regard to their particular aptitudes and abilities
- for continuing the employment of, and arranging appropriate training for, employees who become disabled during their employment with the company
- for the training, career development and promotion of disabled employees.

Failure to do this is a criminal offence by the directors, unless they can show that they took all reasonable steps to ensure that the statement was included. This applies with respect to all 'disabled workers', as defined above, regardless of whether they are registered as such.

Unfair dismissal

Employers should also bear in mind that employees with more than two years' continuous service have the right not to be unfairly dismissed. Dismissal because of incapability is a potentially fair reason for dismissal under section 57(3) of the Employment Protection (Consolidation) Act 1978, and this may apply to the dismissal of disabled employees, as well as to employees dismissed because of ill health. However, even though this is a potentially fair reason for dismissal, employers would be well advised to exercise caution. The fairness of the decision will be judged in the light of all the circumstances of the case, including the size and administrative resources of the employer. Where an employer took on a disabled employee in the full knowledge of their condition, then they would generally be expected to take that disability into account in setting standards for job performance and in giving appropriate training and support. Difficult issues can arise where an employee has failed to disclose a disability when applying for the job but, once employed, their disability becomes apparent. Frequently, the disability will come to the employer's attention before the employee has two years' continuous service, and the employer is then free to dismiss, with appropriate notice, without the need to worry about any unfair dismissal complaint. However, if the disability comes to light after the two-year period, then the employer cannot simply dismiss because the employee failed to disclose their condition.

The employer will either need to justify the dismissal on the grounds of capability or conduct, where the disability affects job performance, or on the ground of 'some other substantial reason'. This latter could apply where the employer has a policy of not employing people with the particular disability in the particular job, and that policy is reasonable in all the circumstances.

If an existing employee develops a disability, then the reasonable employer should first consider what steps can be taken to continue employing the employee. The Employment Service (formerly the Manpower Services Commission) offers various types of assistance for employers, ranging from advice to financial help in providing equipment and adapting premises. However, if the employer feels that there is no alternative to considering dismissal, then it is essential that they follow a fair procedure before taking the decision. There are certain key elements to be considered:

- First, the employer should seek as much information as possible about the nature of the employee's condition. This will usually involve seeking access to the employee's medical records, using the Access to Medical Reports Act 1988. However, the Act gives the employee a right to see any reports from their own doctor before they are disclosed to the employer and to refuse to allow disclosure. It may therefore become vital for the employee to be seen by the company doctor, or a doctor appointed by the employer. However, the employer can only *request* the employee to see such a doctor – unless, of course, there is a clause in the employment contract which allows the employer to require the employee to see a company-nominated doctor.
- Secondly, the employer would be expected to consult with the employee, discussing the nature of the illness, and the likelihood of a return to work.
- Thirdly, the employer should consider whether the employee can be offered alternative employment within the organisation, although there is no obligation to create a new job for the employee. Employers should offer any available alternative work to the disabled employee, even though the new job may not be 'suitable' in terms of status or conditions.

Having followed the appropriate procedural steps, the employer must decide whether or not to dismiss; the tribunals have stressed that this remains a managerial decision, not a medical one.

Health and safety at work

Employers need to bear in mind their general duties under the Health and

Safety at Work etc. Act 1974. So employers, under their general duty to take care of their employees' health and safety, may have to make special provision to ensure the health and safety of disabled workers, by providing them with additional safety protection or equipment. However, the Act also requires employers to consider the health and safety of other workers: this may justify employers moving disabled workers to other jobs, or even dismissing them, if the continued employment of the disabled workers poses a risk to others, or to customers. Employees are also under a duty to take reasonable care of their own health and safety, and that of their fellow workers.

AIDS and HIV

There is evidence of considerable discrimination against people with AIDS or who are HIV-positive. Much of this discrimination is based on ignorance of AIDS and how the disease is spread. The National Aids Trust (NAT) reported in 1993 that they had received over 2,000 legal enquiries, many relating to employment discrimination.[4] Yet there is no specific legal protection. A refusal to employ someone with AIDS, or who is HIV-positive, is not unlawful, and someone who is dismissed for this reason cannot bring an unfair dismissal complaint unless they have two years' continuous service. The NAT found that many dismissed employees were deterred from legal action by the fear of publicity and the costs of bringing a tribunal claim. Even where cases reach a tribunal, employers may be able to show that the dismissal was fair for 'some other substantial reason', such as a refusal by fellow workers, or customers, to continue working with the employee.

The Government has now announced its intention to include those with AIDS and symptomatic HIV in the definition of 'disability' in the Disability Discrimination Bill 1995. This is to be welcomed, and will significantly improve the legal protection for those with AIDS.

Developing policies on disability

With the introduction of legal protection against discrimination on grounds of disability, employers should take steps to review their existing practices, and to introduce and implement a disability policy. The Code of Practice to be issued under the new Bill will be an obvious starting point. The Government has consulted with various organisations, and the Code will contain advice on good practice. In particular, the Code will give guidance on circumstances in which it would be reasonable for employers to make adjustments, and on steps to be taken to prevent employees from doing anything unlawful under the Bill.

Key points

- Be aware of the provisions of the Disability Discrimination Bill and take positive steps to ensure that your organisation complies.
- Ensure that records required under the DP(E)A 1944 are kept.
- Check that the directors' report contains a statement on disability policy.
- When an employee becomes disabled, or disability worsens, consider what can be done to keep the employee in their original job. If this is not possible, consider moving the employee to alternative employment.
- If it is necessary to consider dismissing a disabled employee, obtain as much information as possible about their medical condition. Consult with the employee, and consider alternative employment.
- Keep in mind duties under the Health and Safety at Work etc. Act 1974 with regard to both the health and safety of the disabled employee, and that of others.
- Raise awareness about AIDS and HIV and develop a policy of non-discrimination.
- Take positive steps, through policy development, to encourage recruitment of disabled employees and to ensure that existing employees are given opportunities for training and promotion.

References

1 *Disability, Discrimination and Employment Law*, a Report of the Law Society's Employment Law Committee, November 1992
2 See IRLIB, No. 457, p. 16
3 At the time of writing (late 1995) the Bill had completed the Committee and Report stage in the House of Lords, and was due to receive its Third Reading in the House of Commons at the end of October. The Bill is expected to become law during the autumn of 1995.
4 *HIV and AIDS in the workplace – an examination of cases of discrimination*, Petra Wilson, NAT

Chapter 11
Discrimination on grounds of trade union status

Under UK law there is no right, as such, to trade union membership, but
the law does prohibit discrimination that is due to trade union status. The
current legal position has come about partly as a result of legislation
designed to protect the rights of union members, and partly as a result of
legal initiatives by the Conservative Government designed to end the
'closed shop'. The law now prohibits discrimination on the grounds of
union membership, or non-membership, with respect to recruitment, dismissal and victimisation at work.

Recruitment

Since 1990, it has been unlawful to refuse a person employment because
of their union membership status. This protection was introduced as part
of the Government's measures to outlaw the pre-entry 'closed shop', and
the original Bill granted protection only to people who were refused
employment because they were not members of a union. However, the
Government was persuaded to extend the protection to union members
as well, and Section 137 of the Trade Union and Labour Relations
(Consolidation) Act 1992 (TULR(C)A) provides that it is unlawful to
refuse a person employment:

(a) because he is, or is not, a member of a trade union; or
(b) because he is unwilling to accept a requirement –
   (i) to take steps to become or cease to be, or remain or not to
     become, a member of a trade union; or
   (ii) to make payments or suffer deductions in the event of his not
      being a member of a trade union.

Union membership covers membership in general, or membership of a
particular trade union, or of a particular branch or section of a union.
Employment is 'refused' whenever anyone seeks employment, and the
employer:

• refuses, or deliberately omits to entertain and process the application
  or inquiry

- causes the individual to withdraw or cease to pursue their application or inquiry
- refuses or deliberately omits to offer the individual employment
- makes an offer of employment on terms which no reasonable employer who wished to fill the post would offer, and which is refused
- makes an offer of employment, but withdraws it or causes the applicant not to accept it.

As with sex and race discrimination, it is for the job applicant to prove the reason they were refused employment, and this will often be difficult in practice. However, employers should be aware of two particular situations:

- If a *job advertisement* indicates that employment is only open to union members (or non-members), or that successful applicants will be required to join or leave a union or make payments in lieu, then an applicant who does not satisfy the requirement, or is unwilling to accept the condition, and is refused the job, is *conclusively* presumed to have been refused employment for that reason. Job advertisements are widely defined to include private as well as public notices. So internally advertised vacancies, such as a card on a works notice-board, are covered. It is essential that employers check advertisements to ensure that they contain no indication of any union membership requirements; otherwise, someone who does not satisfy those requirements and who is refused a job has a foolproof claim, regardless of the real reason why they were refused employment.
- Where there is an arrangement or practice whereby jobs are only offered to individuals put forward or *nominated by a trade union*, then a non-union member who is refused employment as a result of that arrangement will be presumed to have been refused employment because they are not a union member. Trade unions themselves, however, can specify union membership when appointing someone to a paid union office.

Similar principles apply to employment agencies who refuse to offer their services to individuals on the grounds of union membership or non-membership.

The TULR(C)A 1992 prohibits discrimination on the grounds of union membership or non-membership. However, it is unclear whether it also covers the situation where an employer has no objection to individuals belonging to a trade union, but refuses to recruit trade union activists (or, indeed, vociferous anti-unionists). The protection for current employees, discussed below, covers both union membership and taking part in trade union activities (or not taking part), whereas the recruitment provisions only refer to union membership. This is a clear difference in wording, and it would appear this was a deliberate decision by the Government. After the House of Lords' decision in *Associated Newspapers Ltd* v. *Wilson*; *Associated British Ports* v. *Palmer* (1995)[1] (see below) it seems employers can refuse employment to a union activist without contravening section 137.

Remedies

The remedy is for the applicant to complain to an industrial tribunal within three months of being refused employment. If the tribunal upholds the claim, they can make a declaration to that effect and a recommendation that the employer take certain steps to obviate or reduce the adverse effect of their actions. But it would seem that the tribunal cannot recommend that the individual be given the next available job. Compensation can be awarded up to the statutory maximum (currently £11,300). This can include an award for injury to feelings. The trade union can be made a party to the action, if either the applicant or the employer alleges that the discrimination occurred because of the threat or use of industrial action. The tribunal can then order the trade union to pay any or all of the compensation awarded.

The right not to be dismissed

Section 152 of the TULR(C)A 1992 makes it automatically unfair to dismiss an employee if the reason, or principal reason, was that the employee:

(a) was, or proposed to become, a member of an independent trade union; or
(b) had taken part, or proposed to take part, in the activities of an independent trade union at an appropriate time; or
(c) was not a member of any trade union, or of a particular trade union, or of one of a number of particular trade unions, or had refused, or proposed to refuse, to become or remain a member.

Unlike ordinary unfair dismissal cases, there is no need for the employee to have two years' continuous employment in order to bring an unfair dismissal case for trade union related grounds. Nor does it matter that the employee has passed the normal retirement age, or is over 65.

The protection covers employees who are dismissed for taking part in trade union activities, as well as for union membership/non-membership. However, the protection only applies to union activities 'at an appropriate time'. This is defined as either outside working hours, or within working hours with the employer's agreement. Working hours are the hours when the employee is actually required to be working – so activities during lunch-hours or tea breaks are outside working hours, even if the employee is paid by the employer and on the employer's premises. Similarly, the time immediately before and after work, when the employee is on the employer's premises, are outside working hours.

During working hours, the employer must have given their consent to the activity. Such consent need not be express and may be established by custom and practice. However, tribunals are reluctant to find that an employer has given implied consent to trade union activities in working time simply because the employer is silent, particularly if the employer does not recognise the trade union.

Trade union activities are not defined, but the case law has established that attending union meetings, participating in union ballots, and consulting union officials are trade union activities, as is recruiting employees into the union. However, there is a fine distinction between trade union activities, and the activities of a trade unionist. In *Chant* v. *Aquaboats Ltd* (1978)[2] Chant, a trade union member, complained about the safety standards of some woodworking machinery, drew up a petition, which he showed to his union official, and then got other employees to sign it. Most of those who signed were not union members. The Employment Appeal Tribunal (EAT) held that this did not make it a union activity. In relation to health and safety matters, however, it should be noted that the Trade Union Reform and Employment Rights Act 1993 now provides protection from unfair dismissal for individuals who take certain actions with respect to health and safety at work.[3]

The protection against dismissal provided by section 152 of the TULR(C)A 1992 only applies to trade union activities during the current employment, not those during past employment. This was established in *Birmingham City District Council* v. *Beyer* (1978).[4] Beyer was a 'notorious union activist' who finally gained a job by concealing his identity. When his true identity was discovered, he was dismissed for his deceit. The EAT accepted this as the true reason for his dismissal, rather than his union activities, but made it clear that, in any event, the protection against dismissal did not cover activities in past employment. However, similar issues arose in *Fitzpatrick* v. *British Railways Board* (1991)[5] and the Court of Appeal reached a different conclusion. Ms Fitzpatrick had been employed by the Ford Motor Company for nine days, but was dismissed when they received bad references. When she applied for a job with British Rail, she did not disclose her employment with Ford. An employee at British Rail read an article in the *Evening Standard* which referred to an employee who was a prominent union activist with ultra-left-wing sympathies, and Miss Fitzpatrick was identified as the employee. British Rail subsequently dismissed her, ostensibly because of the deceit on her application form. However, the Court of Appeal held that the real reason for her dismissal was not the deceit, but her reputation as a union activist. They went on to hold that the employer's real reason for dismissing her, because of her reputation, was not what she had done in the past, but their fear that she would repeat those activities in her current employment. This fell within the statute, which prohibits dismissal on the ground of 'proposed' union activities. The Court of Appeal held that this was an 'almost inevitable' conclusion. Employers should therefore be wary of dismissing union activists already in employment.

Finally, it is clear that 'union activities' do not cover industrial action. An employee who is dismissed while taking part in industrial action is prohibited from bringing an unfair dismissal claim, unless the employer selectively dismisses those taking part, or selectively re-employs within a three-month period.[6] In any event, industrial action will not be a union activity 'at an appropriate time': the employer is unlikely to consent to industrial action, and if it takes place outside working hours the action is unlikely to have much effect.

Remedies

If an employee is dismissed for any of the reasons covered by section 152 of the TULR(C)A 1992, then they can apply to the tribunal for interim relief. An application must be made within seven days, and the tribunal will then hear the case as soon as is reasonably practicable. If the tribunal thinks that the employee's application is likely to succeed, it can order that the employee be reinstated or re-engaged, pending the full hearing of the case. However, the employer has to consent to this. If the employer does not consent, then the tribunal can order continuation of the employee's contract. The effect of this is that the employee is suspended on full pay until the full hearing.

At the full hearing, if the tribunal finds that the employee has been dismissed for a trade union related reason, then the tribunal can make an order for reinstatement or re-engagement. Alternatively, the tribunal can award compensation. In trade union cases, the basic award (a lump sum calculated in the same way as statutory redundancy payments) is subject to a *minimum* of £2,770. The compensatory award is calculated in the same way as other unfair dismissal cases. However, if the employee *requested* reinstatement or re-engagement, but the tribunal did not award reinstatement or re-engagement, then the employee is entitled to a 'special award' of up to 104 weeks' pay, subject to a minimum of £13,775 and a maximum of £27,500. If the tribunal makes an order for reinstatement or re-engagement, but the employer does not comply with this, then the 'special award' is 152 weeks' pay, subject to a minimum of £20,600, but with no maximum. These sums can be reduced where the employee unreasonably refused an offer of re-employment, or where the employee contributed to their own dismissal, but the refusal to join or not to join a union, or not to take part in union activities cannot itself be treated as contributory conduct. Trade union related dismissals can therefore be very expensive for employers, compared with 'ordinary' unfair dismissals.

Victimisation on grounds of trade union status

Section 146(1) of the TULR(C)A 1992 gives employees the right not to have action short of dismissal taken against them as individuals for the purpose of:

(a) preventing or deterring him from being or seeking to become a member of an independent trade union, or penalising him for doing so; or
(b) preventing or deterring him from taking part in the activities of an independent trade union at an appropriate time, or penalising him for doing so; or
(c) compelling him to be or become a member of any trade union or of a particular trade union or of one of a number of particular trade unions.

Action short of dismissal can include transferring the employee to less pleasant work, requiring them to work longer hours, disciplining them, deducting money from their pay, subjecting them to any other detriment, or even refusing them a parking permit.

Difficult issues have arisen over employers offering employees financial incentives to sign individual contracts. In *Wilson* v. *Associated Newspapers* (1993)[7] the *Daily Mail* de-recognised the National Union of Journalists and offered all journalists who signed personal contracts by a certain date a 4.5 per cent pay rise. Those who did not sign did not get the pay rise. Those who signed were free to remain union members. The Court of Appeal ruled that this was a breach of section 146. The employer's purpose in offering a financial incentive in return for giving up rights to union representation and collective bargaining was to deter the employees from remaining members of the union, or penalising them for so doing. There was no genuine distinction between the *rights* of membership and making use of the essential services of a union. The employer's ultimate purpose was to reduce the power of the union and so to deter employees from being members of the union. The Court of Appeal reached a similar conclusion in *Palmer* v. *Associated British Ports* (1993)[8] where employees were offered individual contracts with significant pay rises to those who gave up the right to union representation. The employer continued to negotiate with the union in respect of those employees who did not accept the new contracts. The Court ruled that there was no doubt that the employer's purpose was to persuade employees to abandon union representation so that the union would 'wither on the vine'.

The Government immediately introduced a last-minute amendment to the Trade Union Reform and Employment Rights Bill in order to negate the effect of these two decisions. Section 148(3) of the TULR(C)A 1992 now provides that:

> In determining what was the purpose for which action was taken by the employer against the complainant in a case where -
> (a) there is evidence that the employer's purpose was to further a change in his relationship with all or any class of his employees, and
> (b) there is also evidence that his purpose was one falling within s.146,
> the tribunal shall regard the purpose in paragraph (a) as the purpose for which the employer took the action (and not the purpose mentioned in paragraph (b)), unless it considers that the action was such as no reasonable employer would take.

In other words, in cases like *Wilson* and *Palmer*, the tribunals must ignore any evidence that the employer had an additional purpose of deterring union membership, as well as the immediate purpose of shifting to personal contracts. But the wording of section 148 is potentially much wider, and could include offering pay rises to individuals who join a particular trade union, for example where the employer wishes to introduce a single-union deal. The protection against victimisation has been significantly weakened by the decision of the House of Lords in *Wilson* and *Palmer* (1995)[9.] The Lords overturned the decisions of the Court of Appeal. The Lords held by a majority that the right not to have 'action' short of dismissal taken against an individual did not include any omission to act. In other words, employers who omitted to take action in favour of an employee, such as giving the employee a pay rise, did not contravene section 146(1), regardless of the employer's purpose. The Lords overruled the earlier case of *Ridgeway and Fairbrother* v. *National Coal Board* (1987)[10] where the Court of Appeal had held that it was unlawful for the NCB to award a pay rise to members of the Union of Democratic Mineworkers, but not to members of the National Union of Mineworkers. The result of this decision is that employers can now offer incentives to individuals not only to give up their rights to union representation, but also their right to union membership. As long as the employer does not take any 'action' against the union member, but simply omits to offer them some benefit, then such conduct is lawful.

The House of Lords went on to hold that the protection under section 146(1) was only intended to cover the bare right to belong to a trade union, and this was not to be equated with any right to make use of the union's services. In *Wilson* and *Palmer* the employees were free to remain members of the union. So it would appear that all that is now protected is the bare right to belong to a trade union.

Remedies

An employee who feels they have been unfairly victimised can complain to a tribunal within three months. The tribunal can make a declaration and order such compensation as it thinks just and equitable. This is supposed to compensate the employee, not punish the employer, but tribunals can include sums for injury to feelings.

Key points

- Make sure that any internal or external job advertisements contain no indication that union membership, or non-membership, is a requirement.
- Do not enter into any arrangement whereby jobs are only offered to individuals put forward or nominated by a trade union.
- Do not ask about union membership status on application forms or at interviews.
- Do not make job offers conditional on union membership/non-membership.
- Do not dismiss employees for union-related reasons.
- Do not take action short of dismissal against individuals for union-related reasons.

References

1 [1995] IRLR 258
2 [1978] 3 All ER 102
3 See new section 22A, EP(C)A 1978
4 [1978] 1 All ER 910
5 [1991] IRLR 376
6 See EP(C)A 1978, ss. 237–8
7 [1993] IRLR 336
8 [1993] IRLR 336
9 [1995] IRLR 258

Chapter 12
Ex-offenders

There is evidence of considerable discrimination against ex-offenders. Much of this discrimination occurs in recruitment, as many employers are unwilling to take on someone with a criminal record. Whilst there are obviously certain offences which make individuals unsuitable for particular kinds of employment, in many cases employers exhibit a blanket prejudice against applicants with any criminal record. As with other forms of discrimination, such a prejudice prevents employers from making recruitment decisions on the basis of merit. Employers should therefore consider including ex-offenders in their equal opportunities policy and establishing appropriate recruitment guidelines.

The Rehabilitation of Offenders Act 1974

The purpose of the Rehabilitation of Offenders Act 1974 is that ex-offenders should be able to put their criminal record behind them after a certain period of rehabilitation. The criminal record then becomes 'spent', and the individual need not disclose it to a prospective employer.

The length of the rehabilitation period varies according to the sentence imposed. So, for example, where an individual receives a prison sentence of between 6 and 30 months, the rehabilitation period is 10 years. The period begins at the date of the conviction. The detail of the rehabilitation periods is contained in section 5 of the Act. But, in general terms, any sentence of 2¹/₂ years or more cannot become 'spent' under the terms of the Act.

Once a conviction is 'spent', then the individual is to be treated 'for all purposes in law as a person who has not committed or been charged with or prosecuted for or convicted of or sentenced for the offence'. Under section 4(2), where an individual is asked about previous convictions they are entitled to treat the question as not relating to the spent conviction. So if an employer asks a job applicant about any previous convictions, either on an application form or at interview, then the applicant does not need to reveal the 'spent' convictions. Employers have sometimes tried to argue that employees are in breach of contract for failing to disclose 'spent' convictions – either under an express contractual term, or as a breach of an implied term of mutual trust and understanding.

These arguments have not succeeded. Section 4(2)(b) provides that a person 'shall not be subjected to any liability or otherwise prejudiced in law' because they failed to disclose a 'spent' conviction. Section 4 also makes it clear that it is not only the fact of the conviction which need not be disclosed, but also all the surrounding circumstances of the offence itself.

Dismissal and refusal to offer a job

Section 4(3) provides that a 'spent' conviction shall not be a proper ground for dismissing or excluding someone from a job. So even if an applicant does tell the employer about a 'spent' conviction, the employer cannot use this as a ground for refusing employment. Similarly, it is not lawful for an employer to dismiss someone, or fail to offer them a job, simply because they failed to disclose a 'spent' conviction, or indeed any of the circumstances surrounding the offence. It is also unlawful to 'prejudice' an employee in any way because of a spent conviction, and this would cover demotion, refusal of promotion, or any other detrimental treatment.

Unfortunately for the ex-offender, the Act does not provide any specific remedies. It is clear that where an employee is dismissed for a reason connected with a spent conviction, then this will be an unfair dismissal, but the employee must still have two years' continuous service in order to be able to bring an action. If an employee is prejudiced in some way, then they could resign and claim constructive dismissal. However, where an applicant is refused employment, then it may be difficult for them to obtain compensation for this, as the Act makes no specific provision for compensation, and it is unlikely that the employer would be ordered to offer the applicant the job.

Provision of references

If an employer is asked to write a reference, they are not obliged to give details of any 'spent' convictions, and any failure by a referee to disclose 'spent' convictions cannot give rise to legal liability. Indeed, disclosure of 'spent' convictions will be deemed unlawful if the referee has acted with 'malice' – 'some irrelevant, spiteful, or improper motive'.[1] As mentioned above, an employer who receives references containing details of a 'spent' conviction will be acting unlawfully if they refuse the applicant a job for this reason.

Exceptions

There are a number of exceptions, where the provisions of the Act do not apply. These are contained in the Rehabilitation of Offenders Act 1974 (Exceptions) Order 1975 and include doctors, dentists, nurses and midwives, opticians, pharmacists, workers in the social services, teachers and youth workers, the police, the prison service, traffic wardens, lawyers and judges. The Secretary of State can add to the list, last revised in 1986. For these jobs, applicants can be asked to reveal 'spent' convictions and can be refused employment, or dismissed, because of the conviction or the failure to disclose it.

If a job is not listed, then the usual rules apply – even if it seems to the employer that disclosure should be necessary. In *Property Guards Ltd* v. *Taylor and Kershaw* (1982)[2] two security guards were dismissed when the employer discovered that they had spent convictions for dishonesty. They had signed a statement saying that they had never been convicted of any criminal offences. The employer argued that the nature of the job put them under a special duty to disclose any conviction, spent or otherwise. The EAT held the dismissals were unfair: unless the Secretary of State exempts employment, then the employer cannot dismiss because of 'spent' convictions, regardless of the nature of the job.

'Unspent' convictions

There is no general duty on job applicants to disclose past convictions. It is only where the employer asks the applicant directly about past criminal offences that the applicant is under any duty to come clean about 'unspent' convictions. If the applicant dishonestly conceals past offences, then this may justify a dismissal when the employer discovers the truth. However, it is not automatically fair to dismiss an employee because of a deliberate dishonesty about a past conviction: everything will depend on the circumstances, including the nature of the offence, how long ago it occurred, whether it is related to the job in any way, and the employee's employment record. In particular, employers should be careful to follow a fair procedure before dismissing. Again, individuals must have two years' continuous employment before they are eligible to begin unfair dismissal proceedings.

Pre-recruitment checks

Employers should also be aware that, in relation to certain kinds of employment, it may be necessary to carry out checks to see whether the applicant has any previous convictions. Where the job is listed in the Exemption Order, then this can include checking for 'spent' convictions as well as 'unspent' ones. There are procedures for making checks using police and court records, regulated by the Home Office, and there are also commercial agencies who carry out vetting procedures – although employers should be careful to ensure the accuracy of such checks wherever possible. Employers who fail to check up on references, or the information given by the applicant, could be sued for negligence if an individual suffers some loss or damage as a result.

Key points

- Consider including ex-offenders within an equal opportunities policy.
- Examine recruitment practices to ensure that ex-offenders are not routinely discriminated against.
- Where a criminal offence comes to light during the recruitment process, check whether it is 'spent' under the Rehabilitation of Offenders Act 1974. If it is, ignore it. If not, examine whether it really makes the applicant unsuitable for the job in question.
- Where it is later discovered that an employee has a 'spent' conviction, do not use this, or the failure to disclose it, as a reason for dismissing the employee or subjecting them to any other detriment.
- When writing references, do not give details of any spent convictions, unless the job is covered by the Exemption Order (this should be clearly stated on the reference request).
- Where an 'unspent' conviction comes to light, do not automatically dismiss. Consider whether it is job related and, in any event, ensure that all appropriate procedural steps are taken.

References

1 *Herbage* v. *Pressdram Ltd* [1984] 2 All ER 769
2 [1982] IRLR 175

Chapter 13
Taking non-discrimination further:
equal opportunities policies

The focus of this book has been on the legal aspects of non-discrimination: what employers and organisations can or cannot do within the current state of the law on sex and race discrimination, equal pay and other areas. The law in this area is complex, fast-changing and developing into new areas all the time: organisations have to work hard at simply ensuring that they stay within the law. The law is a very important tool in fighting discrimination: as can be seen with disability discrimination, a policy of simply encouraging employers to adopt 'good practice' is generally ineffective without the 'stick' of legal sanctions. But law alone will not bring about equal opportunities. However, even within existing legislation, organisations are encouraged to go behind a strategy of trying not to break the law, but instead to develop policies that promote greater equality of opportunity within the workforce. The CRE and the EOC both have Codes of Practice, which tribunals can, and do, take into account, and which encourage the development of equal opportunities policies; the EOC has also published a detailed draft Code of Practice on developing an Equal Pay policy. The European Commission has issued a Code of Practice on Sexual Harassment, the CRE has issued guidance on how to implement a racial harassment policy, and the development of a Code of Practice is a key element of the new disability discrimination legislation.

There are other reasons why organisations should develop such policies. It is important to make people realise that equal opportunities can be a sound business objective rather than just 'politically correct'. Unfair discrimination involves taking account of irrelevant factors in decision-making and can lead to the wrong decision being made. Recruitment policies which have a discriminatory impact may mean that the organisation is not getting the best person for the job; lack of training opportunities can mean that the organisation is wasting the potential of its workforce. The climate within an organisation can make the difference between good and poor levels of staff retention. The CRE has stated that there are many benefits to business from promoting racial equality, including getting closer to customers and their needs, improving international success, and making the company more attractive to investors.[1] There is a strong argument that avoiding unfair discrimination is good for business. But the law can also be a useful element in persuading individuals to take equal opportunities seriously. Since the ceiling was lifted on compensation levels for sex and race discrimination, legal action can prove very expensive, and senior managers may pay more attention to the possibility of costly law suits than to the mere assertion that equal opportunities is good for business.

The introduction of the new Disability Discrimination legislation will provide a useful reason for companies to reassess existing policies, and to consider how equal opportunities within organisations can be improved. In particular, the scope of existing policies will have to be reassessed: many organisations have policies that cover sex and race, but a real commitment to equal opportunities will involve examining the extent of discrimination on grounds of disability, sexuality, age, religion, family responsibilities and other factors. It has been suggested that the current focus of equal opportunities policies is itself misplaced: that instead of concentrating on groups of workers who fall within a particular category, employers should instead look at *all* the individuals within an organisation (including white middle-class men!) to see whether they are fulfilling their potential. The advantage of this approach is that it includes everybody within its scope and concentrates on the *diversity* of all individuals within an organisation, rather than just looking at a woman worker as a woman.[2] Family-friendly policies, for example, should examine men's problems in reconciling work and family life, as well as women's. This approach can feed into a good equal opportunities policy by concentrating on the advantages to everyone rather than by simply avoiding disadvantages to particular groups.

What is a good equal opportunities policy?

There are many specialist books offering detailed guidance on how to establish and maintain an equal opportunities policy.[3] There are also many specialist forms of guidance dealing specifically with such issues as race, disability, age discrimination and sexuality. Organisations will vary enormously in their requirements, according to their size, administrative resources, location and the nature of their business. There are however certain key points that apply to all organisations.

Firstly, the most significant element in making equal opportunities work is a commitment to the aims of the policy throughout the organisation, and especially from the top management. Equal opportunities is too often sidelined as simply a personnel issue; it is important that it is widened out so that everyone is involved (and particularly managers) in thinking about what equal opportunities means in every aspect of their job. Drafting an equal opportunities policy should not be left to the personnel or human resource division alone. Here, the approach of focusing on managing diversity, rather than simple non-discrimination, can be important, as is an awareness of the possible business advantages to the whole organisation.

Secondly, the organisation should undertake an equal opportunities audit in order to see where any problems lie. This will involve looking at all aspects of the employment relationship: recruitment, training, promotion, dismissal, redundancy, staff turnover, and pay structures. The importance of record-keeping and monitoring cannot be overemphasised here. Unless an organisation has the necessary statistical information it is impossible to identify where discrimination is occurring. All the factors included in the concept of equal opportunities should be monitored, not just sex and race. The monitoring should cover all applicants for jobs, candidates for internal promotions, those who are given training opportunities, those selected for redundancy and dismissal, and also staff who leave voluntarily. The pay structure needs to be analysed in terms of these factors too.

Once the audit has been carried out, an indication of potential problems within the organisation should emerge. The focus should then shift to how to address those problems. In addition to developing an overall strategy, specific solutions should be sought for specific problems. For example, the company may have a very poor record of women returning to work after maternity leave. Why? What can be done to improve the position? Is turnover higher amongst women or ethnic minorities? In either case, is this because of a lack of opportunity for career development? Does the selection process produce fewer non-white applicants than would statistically be predicted for the locality? If so, is it because the company relies on word-of-month recruitment, or advertises in ways that do not reach ethnic minorities, or has a poor reputation for employing non-whites? Are older workers stuck in terms of career development? If so, is this because they are not offered training opportunities available to younger workers? Are there age limits set for recruitment that are not strictly necessary for the job? How many disabled workers are there within the organisation, and at what levels? Where existing workers become disabled, does the company actively seek to retain them by offering support and flexible working arrangements? There may be many other issues revealed by an equal opportunities audit. It is important to realise, furthermore, that monitoring should be continuous: the problems, and the solutions required, will change over time.

The action taken should go further than simply addressing specific problems. The development of an effective policy will involve setting up a clear structure of responsibility for equal opportunities, and this is likely to be more effective if all individuals within the organisation are involved in thinking about equal opportunities. This is particularly important for all those in managerial positions. Rather than having an Equal Opportunities Officer in the Personnel Department – though this may be an important and necessary role – all managers should be involved in, and receive training in, equal opportunities policies. The culture of the organisation may need to change, which can happen only if there is effective and committed leadership.

Those involved in drafting the policies should also consider whether to offer positive opportunities for underrepresented groups or individuals, and in particular whether they wish to take advantage of the limited scope for positive discrimination in training permitted under the RRA 1976 and the SDA 1975. (See Chapters 4 and 7.) It may also be useful to set objectives and timetables for improving recruitment, retention, or promotion of particular groups, and to give managers specific responsibilities for reporting on progress and the steps taken to achieve those targets.

Once an equal opportunities policy has been introduced, the most important step in ensuring that it is effective is continuous monitoring of the policy: this is essential to ensure that potential deficiencies and drawbacks are spotted. An equal opportunities policy should be seen as a living thing that can grow and develop over time. The policy should be regularly assessed and reviewed, with procedures in place for changing it when necessary. It is important that everyone within the organisation feels involved in this process: a system of consultation and feedback should be incorporated into the policy.

Conclusion

Thousands of organisations boldly proclaim themselves to be 'An Equal Opportunities Employer' on job advertisements, but the evidence from the tribunals suggests that not all of these employers take the matter seriously. Employers should realise that it is not enough to draft a model policy on equal opportunities and then leave it to gather dust in the personnel department. Research commissioned by the CRE found that almost 90 per cent of large companies surveyed had racial equality policies, but only 45 per cent of those companies had taken any steps to implement the policy.[4] A real commitment to equal opportunities involves a willingness to address problems within the organisation, to get everyone involved, and to monitor constantly the effectiveness of the policy.

Key Points

- Maintain awareness of legal developments.
- Be aware of Codes of Practice issued under discrimination legislation.

- Increase awareness that non-discrimination offers business advantages.
- Examine existing policies.
- Consider using the diversity of all employees, not just those in disadvantaged groups.
- Be aware of specialist literature on equal opportunities.
- Ensure commitment throughout the organisation.
- Undertake an equal opportunity audit, involving record-keeping and monitoring.
- Find specific solutions for specific problems.
- Involve everyone in the development of an equal opportunities policy.
- Consider positive action and setting objectives.
- Ensure continuous monitoring and assessment of the policy.

References

1 *Racial Equality Means Business: A standard for racial equality for employers'*, CRE, 1995
2 See *Managing the Mosaic: Diversity in action*, R. Kandola and J. Fullerton, London, IPD, 1994
3 See, for example, *Making Equal Opportunities Work*, M. Coussey and H. Jackson, London, Pitman, 1991, and *Equality Matters: Equal opportunities in the 90s*, H. Collins, London, Library Association, 1992
4 *Large Companies and Racial Equality*, CRE, 1995

List of cases

AC	Appeal Cases
All ER	All England Law Reports
COIT	Central Office of Industrial Tribunals
EOR-DCLD	Equal Opportunities Review – Discrimination Case Law Digest
ICR	Industrial Cases Reports
IDS	Incomes Data Services Ltd
IRLB	Industrial Relations Law Bulletin
IRLIB	Industrial Relations Legal Information Bulletin
IRLR	Industrial Relations Law Reports
QB	Queen's Bench
TLR	Times Law Reports
WLR	Weekly Law Reports

Ahmad v. *ILEA* [1977] ICR 490   101

Arnold v. *Beecham Group Ltd* [1982] IRLR 307   69

Associated Newspapers Ltd v. *Wilson; Associated British Ports* v. *Palmer* [1995] IRLR 258   125

Aziz v. *Trinity Street Taxis Ltd* [1988] IRLR 204   40, 94

Barber v. *Guardian Royal Exchange Assurance Group* [1990] IRLR 240   62, 82, 83

Barber v. *NCR (Manufacturing) Ltd* [1993] IRLR 95   77

Beneveniste v. *Southampton University* [1989] IRLR 122   80

Biggs v. *Somerset County Council* [1995] IRLR 452   4, 82

Bilka-Kaufhaus GmbH v. *Weber von Hartz* [1986] IRLR 317   12, 75, 81, 86, 93

Birmingham City District Council v. *Beyer* [1978] 1 All ER 910   126

BP Chemicals Ltd v. *Gillick and Roevin Management Services Ltd* [1995] IRLR 128   16

Bracebridge Engineering Ltd v. *Darby* [1990] IRLR 3   34

British Coal Corporation v. *Smith; North Yorkshire County Council* v. *Ratcliffe* [1994] IRLR 343   65, 66, 71–2

British Railways Board v. *Paul* [1989] IRLR 20   63

Bromley v. *H & J Quick Ltd* [1987] IRLR 456   71

Brook v. *London Borough of Haringey* [1992] IRLR 478   13, 31

Bullock v. *Alice Ottley School* [1992] IRLR 564   32

Capper Pass Ltd v. *Lawton* [1977] QB 852   67

Chant v. *Aquaboats Ltd* [1978] 3 All ER 102   126

Charles Early and Marriot (Witney) Ltd v. *Smith and Ball* [1977] IRLR 123   80

List of statutes and regulations

British legislation

Access to Medical Reports Act 1988   120
Criminal Justice and Public Order Act 1994   106
Disability Discrimination Bill 1995   115, 116, 118, 121
Disabled Persons (Employment) Act 1944   115, 121
Disabled Persons (Employment) Act 1958   115
Education Act 1944   102
Employment Act 1989   26
Employment Protection (Consolidation) Act 1978   3, 31, 44, 46, 48, 49, 50, 119
Equal Pay Act 1970   2, 6, 21, 61, 63, 64, 66, 68, 69, 75, 81
Fair Employment (Northern Ireland) Act 1989   110
Health and Safety at Work etc. Act 1974   120, 122
Pensions Act 1995   84
Race Relations Act 1976   17, 40, 87, 89, 93, 95, 96, 98, 100, 101,103, 104, 109,
   111
Race Relations Remedies Act 1994   106
Rehabilitation of Offenders Act 1974   131–134
Sex Discrimination Act 1975   6, 7, 9, 14, 16, 17, 18, 21, 22, 23, 26, 27, 29, 30, 31,
   32, 34, 40, 55, 56, 58, 63, 64, 81, 93, 95, 100, 103, 111
Sex Discrimination Act 1986   26, 63
Social Security Act 1975   81
Social Security Act 1989   44, 82
Trade Union and Labour Relations (Consolidation) Act 1992   123, 124, 126,
   127, 128, 129
Trade Union Reform and Employment Rights Act 1993   37, 44, 46, 53, 54

Companies (Directors' Reports) (Employment of Disabled Persons) Regulations
   1980   118
Employment Protection (Part-Time Employees) Regulations 1995   3, 6
Equal Pay (Amendment) Regulations 1983   62
Equal Value Regulations   72
Industrial Tribunals (Rules of Procedure) Regulations 1985   73
Industrial Tribunals (Rules of Procedure) Regulations 1993   73
Management of Health and Safety at Work (Amendment) Regulations 1994   53
Occupational Pension Schemes (Equal Access to Membership) Regulations
   1995   64, 82
Rehabilitation of Offenders Act 1974 (Exceptions) Order 1975   133, 134
Sex Discrimination and Equal Pay (Remedies) Regulations 1993   14

European legislation

Index